SPECTRUM

Writing

Grade 3

SPECTRUM

Columbus, Ohio

Credits:
School Specialty Publishing Editorial/Art & Design Team
Vincent F. Douglas, *President*
Tracey E. Dils, *Publisher*
Jennifer Blashkiw Pawley, *Project Editor*
Suzanne M. Diehm, *Project Editor*
Rose Audette, *Art Director*

Contributors:
Mary Waugh
Holly Fitzgerald
Dr. Betty Jane Wagner
Kris Robinson-Cobb
Theresa Gerig
Glenda Sible Shull
Virginia Allison

Also Thanks to:
Illustrated Alaskan Moose Inc., *Cover Illustration*
4ward Communications, *Interior Design and Production*
Mike Dammer, *Interior Illustration*

Send all inquiries to:
School Specialty Publishing
8720 Orion Place
Columbus, OH 43240-2111

ISBN 1-57768-913-5

8 9 10 11 12 13 POH 11 10 09 08 07 06

Table of Contents

Table of Contents

Creative Writing

Writing Paragraphs

Writing Better Sentences

Writing Letters

Things to Remember About Writing

Prewriting

- Brainstorm topics you might like to write about.
- Create a list of things you could write about each topic.
- Choose the topic you know the most about and that would be of interest to others.
- Collect information.

Writing

- Use sentences in a paragraph only if they tell about the main idea of the paragraph.
- Write directions for doing something in proper order.
- Remember to use sequence words like *first*, *next*, and *last* to put events in the proper order.
- Use *er* or *est*, *more* or *most* to compare things.
- Use details to tell how something looks, sounds, smells, tastes, or feels.
- Think about your purpose before you start writing.
- Write a rough draft focusing on what you want to say rather than the spelling, punctuation, and grammar. You will have the opportunity to make corrections later.

Revising

- Read your rough draft, making changes for interest and clarity.
- Use words that are exact to make your sentences clear.
- Be sure every sentence has a subject and a verb.
- Combine sentences to make your writing smoother.
- Make all verbs in a paragraph or story tell about the same time (verb tense).
- Ask a parent or friend to read your writing and offer suggestions for improvement.

Proofreading

Check to see that:
- you used capital letters correctly.
- you put in correct punctuation marks.
- you used proper grammar.
- all words are spelled correctly.
- you used correct verb forms.

Proofreading Checklist

Use this checklist when proofreading your writing. It will help you remember things you may forget as you review your work.

- [x] Does each sentence being with a capital letter and end with a period, question mark, or exclamation point? *yes*
- [ ] Does each sentence have a subject and verb and a complete thought?
- [ ] Are there any fragments or run-on sentences?
- [ ] Are all words capitalized that should be?
- [ ] Are all words spelled correctly?
- [ ] Have you used troublesome verbs? If so, have you used the correct forms?
- [ ] Does each subject agree with its verb?
- [ ] Did you choose exact words to make your writing clear?
- [ ] Does each pronoun agree with the word it refers to?
- [ ] Have you used apostrophes correctly - to show contractions or possessives?
- [ ] Have all necessary commas been correctly inserted?
- [ ] Have you checked the grammar and usage in your writing?
- [ ] Have you indented your paragraphs?

Proofreading Marks

Use these proofreading marks to help you make corrections in your writing. Try to use a colored pencil or pen when you proofread so that your marks will stand out.

≡	capital letter	Max smith
/	lowercase letter	We like to Eat…
⊙	add period	It was fun
?	add question mark	Do you like pizza
∧	insert, add this	Ten people were coming…
℘	delete, take out	Jump all around
∨	add apostrophe	The bike was Sarahs.
¶	new paragraph	happy. ¶The boy…
∩	transpose, switch the order	the childs toy
∧	add a comma	hiking, biking fishing
⬭	check spelling	I didn't beleive her.

Capitalization
Sentences, People, and Pets

- The first word in a sentence is capitalized.
    Basketball is fun to play.
    Where is my basketball?

- The word **I** is capitalized.
    Do you think **I** can make a basket from here?

- The names of people and pets are capitalized.
    Monica **W**ilson is the coach of our basketball team.
    Carlos is the best player on our team.
    We met **P**atty and **L**isa at the game.
    My cat, **B**oots, likes to play with a ball of yarn.

Practice

Read the sentences below. From each pair of words in parentheses, choose the correct word and circle it.

1. (Basketball, basketball) is a fast and exciting sport.

2. In 1891 (james naismith, James Naismith) invented the game.

3. Ted and (i, I) practice our jump shots after school.

4. My dog, (Tipper, tipper), watches us shoot baskets in the backyard.

5. (the, The) Chicago Bulls is a championship team.

6. (michael Jordan, Michael Jordan) was my favorite player in the NBA.

Capitalization
People's Titles

- Names showing how you are related to someone are capitalized only if they are used in place of or as part of the relative's name.

    Fishing is **G**randpa's favorite hobby.
    Every summer, my **g**randpa takes us fishing.
    Last year, my **m**om caught a huge fish.
    This year, **M**om caught only a cold.

- Titles of respect used with names of persons are capitalized.

    Dr. Elizabeth Blackwell   **M**rs. Alvarez
    President Bush   **M**r. Peter Tepper
    Our class wrote letters to **M**ayor Busby.
    Our teacher, **M**s. Whitley, knows the mayor.

Practice

Read each pair of sentences. Underline the sentence that has the correct capitalization.

1. My Uncle has the same name as an American symbol.
   His name is Uncle Sam.

2. *The Cat in the Hat* was written by dr. Seuss.
   He was not really a doctor.

3. In *The Wizard of Oz*, Dorothy called out, "Auntie Em."
   At the same time, her aunt worried about her.

4. A main character in *Peter Pan* was Captain Hook.
   He was the mean Captain of a pirate ship.

Capitalization
Places

- The major words in geographical names are capitalized.

Chicago	**A**rizona	**I**taly
Ohio **R**iver	**M**ount **R**ushmore	**P**acific **O**cean
Lake **H**uron	**A**sia	

We flew directly from **L**yon, **F**rance, to **M**anchester, **E**ngland.
The **R**io **G**rande flows from the **S**an **J**uan **M**ountains of **C**olorado to the **G**ulf of **M**exico.

- The names of roads, places, and buildings are capitalized.

Fairmont **A**venue	**H**erald **S**quare
Washington **M**onument	**W**hite **H**ouse

The **S**ears **T**ower is taller than the **E**mpire **S**tate **B**uilding.
Columbia **H**ospital is on **C**entral **A**venue.

Practice

Rewrite the sentences. Look for two words in each sentence that should be capitalized.

1. We're planning to take a trip throughout north america.

   <u>We're planning to tak a trip thro ughout North Amerika to America</u>

2. My mom works at broadview hospital.

   <u>My mom works at Broadview Hospi tall</u>

3. My older brother wants to hike through the grand canyon.

   <u>My older brother wants to hike through the grand canyon.</u>

Capitalization
Dates and Holidays

- The names of the days of the week and the months of the year are capitalized.
Monday	**W**ednesday	**S**aturday
April	**J**uly	**O**ctober

  Mai goes to the library every **T**uesday afternoon.
  The hottest days of the summer are often in **J**uly.

- The names of holidays are capitalized.
Labor **D**ay	**T**hanksgiving	**P**residents' **D**ay

  Flag **D**ay is celebrated on June 14.
  I look forward to **C**olumbus **D**ay every year.

- The names of the four seasons of the year are not capitalized
spring	**s**ummer	**f**all	**w**inter

Practice

Read the sentences below. If the underlined part contains an error in capitalization, circle the word or words that should be capitalized.

We honor Americans who gave their lives for our country on <u>Memorial day</u>. Memorial Day is celebrated on the last <u>monday</u> in <u>may</u>. Some people call this holiday <u>decoration day</u>. Flowers and flag are placed on the graves of military personnel in <u>spring</u>. Many towns have parades on Memorial Day and <u>independence day</u> to honor people who served our country.

Proofreading Practice:
Commas

As you read about the colors of the flag of the United States, you will notice all the commas have been left out. Read the sentences carefully. Use the proofreader's mark (∧) to show where commas need to be added.

The Red, White, and Blue

Who made the first flag of the United States? No one really knows. A common belief is that Betsy Ross designed the first flag of the United States. She lived in Philadephia∧Pennsylvania. A man named Francis Hopkinson claimed he designed the first one. Actually∧this argument has never been settled, but historians do not believe Betsy Ross was the designer.

Why is our flag red∧white∧and blue? There is no record of why the Continental Congress chose these colors. They seem appropriate since red is for courage∧white is for purity∧and blue is for justice∧and perseverance. The stripes stand for the original 13 colonies. The number of stars on the flag represents states admitted to the Union. As new states joined the Union∧additional stars were added. At the present time there are 50 stars representing the 50 states. The 50th star represents Hawaii. On August 21∧1959 Hawaii was the last state to join the Union.

Possessives
Singular

- A **possessive noun** shows ownership or a relationship between two things. An apostrophe (') is always used to mark possessive nouns.

    Jane**'s** mountain bike is blue.

    The windowsill is the cat**'s** favorite place to sleep.

- A **singular possessive noun** shows ownership by one person or thing.

    Gary**'s** locker   the principal**'s** office

- To make a singular noun possessive, just add **'s**.

    the smile of the baby—the baby**'s** smile

Practice

On each line below, write the possessive form of the word in parentheses.

1. This is the house that Jack built. Is this _____ house? (Jack)

2. Mary has a garden. How does _____ garden grow? (Mary)

3. Little Boy Blue, come blow your horn. The _____ flute broke. (girl)

4. Jack jumped over the candlestick. Did the _____ flame hurt? (candle)

5. A wise old owl lived in an oak. Is the tree really the _____ home? (owl)

6. Little Miss Muffet sat on a tuffet. Where was the _____ chair? (girl)

Possessives
Singular and Plural

- A **singular possessive noun** shows ownership by one person or thing.
    the **ship's** captain   the **sailor's** uniform

- A **plural possessive noun** shows ownership by more than one person or thing.
    the **cities'** streets   the **states'** governors

- To make a plural noun that ends in **s** a possessive noun, add only the apostrophe.
    Girls—girls'   schools—schools'

- To make a plural noun that does not end in **s** a possessive noun, add an apostrophe and **s**.
    children—children**'s**   teeth—teeth**'s**

Practice

Change the underlined words to include a plural possessive noun. The first one is done for you.

sea otters' faces

1. The cameras show the <u>faces of the sea otters</u>.

2. Otters sometimes play by sliding down the <u>slopes of the riverbanks</u>.

3. The <u>mother of pups</u> watches them as they play.

4. The mother otter cracks open the <u>shells of sea urchins for food</u>.

5. She grooms the <u>coats of the babies</u> to keep them clean and waterproof.

Proofreading Practice:
Possessives

As you read the stories below, you will notice that apostrophes have not been added to show possessives. Read the sentences carefully. Use the proofreader's mark (∨) to show where apostrophes need to be added. For extra practice, use the proofreader's mark (≡) to correct the capitalization.

The Pet Parade

parkersville fun festival was held each year during the first two weeks in june. There were always a lot of fun activities. They included all sorts of contests, games, and carnival rides.

the parkersville pet parade was held on the first saturday of the festival. All the neighborhood kids pets were ready for the parade. adams turtle had a picture of the united states flag painted on its back. kristens kitten, caramel, had a baby bonnet tied around its head and kept trying to get it off. ryans collie had been brushed until its coat sparkled, and it didn't mind the leash at all. justins bird was riding in its cage on the wagon justin had decorated. gabes llama was probably the most unusual pet of all. he hoped to win first prize.

Contractions
With *Not*

- A contraction is a shortened form of two words that are joined together. When the words are contracted, some letters are left out. An apostrophe takes the place of the letters that have been left out.

    My bicycle **does not** work. My bicycle **doesn't** work.

- Many contractions are made by putting together a verb and the word **not**.

    did not—did**n't**   are not—are**n't**
    do not—do**n't**   was not—was**n't**
    have not—have**n't**   could not—could**n't**
    has not—has**n't**   should not—should**n't**

- Two exceptions are:

    cannot—ca**n't**   will not—wo**n't**

Practice

Write a contraction above the underlined words in each sentence.

We <u>are not</u> smiling. The car <u>will not</u> start, and the mechanic <u>cannot</u>

fix it until Friday. Antonia <u>could not</u> go to her piano lesson. Raphael

<u>was not</u> able to go to baseball practice. I <u>have not</u> gone to the library

to work on my report. We probably <u>should not</u> blame "Old Betsy."

Contractions
With *Verbs*

- Some contractions are formed by joining the words I, you, she, he, it, we, or they with a verb.

I + am = I'm   we + are = we're
I + have = I've   we + have = we've
he + is = he's   you + are = you're
she + is = she's they + are = they're
it + is = it's   they + will = they'll
she + will = she'll

Practice

Write the letter of the words in Column B that matches the contraction in Column A.

Column A	Column B
_____ 1. I'm	a. you are
_____ 2. they're	b. I have
_____ 3. you're	c. we are
_____ 4. I've	d. it is
_____ 5. we're	e. they are
_____ 6. it's	f. she will
_____ 7. she'll	g. I am

Homophones
Hear/Here, To/Too/Two

- Words that sound alike but are spelled differently and have different meanings are called **homophones**.

- *Hear* and *here* are homophones. **Hear** means "to listen to something." **Here** means "at" or "in this place." A good way to remember the difference is that **hear** has an "ear" in it.
    Can you **hear** it ring?
    I am going to put the telephone over **here**.

- Another example is **to**, **too**, and **two**. To means "toward." **Too** means "also" or" more than enough." **Two** is the number between one and three.
    Maggie and Theresa went **to** the movies and ate **two** bags of popcorn. They drank lemonade, **too**.

Practice

Write the correct homophone in each sentence below.

1. "I'm going _____ the tennis court," Meg announced. (too, to, two)

2. Her younger sister, Peg, asked, "May I go, _____ ?" (too, to, two)

3. Meg said, "Sure, tennis is a game for _____ people." (too, to, two)

4. Meg added, _____ , you may use my old racket." (Here, Hear)

5. Peg asked, "Do you _____ Mom calling us?" (hear, here)

Articles

A, an, and the

- **A**, **an**, and **the** are useful words called <u>articles</u>. You can think of them as noun signals. They tell the reader there is a noun coming in the sentence.

- **A** and **an** tell about any person, place, thing, or idea.

- Use **a** with nouns that start with a consonant.
  a ball   **a** jump rope   **a** zebra

- Use **an** with nouns that start with a vowel sound.
  an egg   **an** oyster   **an** umbrella

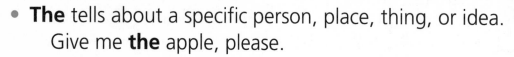

- **The** tells about a specific person, place, thing, or idea.
  Give me **the** apple, please.

Practice

Underline each word (article) in the sentences below that signals any person, place, thing, or idea. Circle each word (article) that signals a specific person, place, thing, or idea.

> We took my brother Jim to college last week. I had never been to a big university before. The campus was as big as a small town. Jim has classes in several different buildings. We visited a science building and the library. The dormitory where Jim lives is a ten-story building. The cafeteria and study rooms are on the first floor. The computer lab is on the fifth floor.

Recognizing Sentences

A sentence is a group of words that tells a whole idea.
A student has accidentally erased some of the words on the board.
Look at each group of words.

Is it still a sentence? Write **yes** or **no** in the ☐ .

Weekly Plans

☐ We will finish our science project by Friday.

☐ This week's class helpers

☐ Please turn in your book report by Thursday.

☐ Don't forget to

☐ Try to read for fifteen minutes at home each night.

☐ We will study fractions in math this week.

☐ We will see a film about

☐ Our weekly reading project will be

☐ Sign up for Sports Day.

☐ Our guest speaker is

☐ Our math review is Wednesday.

☐ Leave your desk neat each day.

Choose **two** of the **no** lines. Add words to make complete sentences.

1. _____

2. _____

Making Sentences

A sentence must tell a complete thought. Read the sentence parts. Draw a line to match each correct beginning and ending.

1. John and Patty attend   for two fun-filled weeks.

2. The band camp lasts   and Patty plays the flute.

3. All the kids bring   practice music together.

4. John plays the tuba,   a band camp every summer.

5. Each day the kids   they give a final concert.

6. The teacher helps them   improve their performance.

7. On the last day,   their own instruments.

Writing Sentences

A sentence must make sense. Read each
sentence. Put an X on the two words which
do not belong. Write the correct sentence
on the line.

1. Last Saturday I night helped Granddad clean his phone attic.

_____

_____

2. We found extra three old trunks covered with place cobwebs.

_____

_____

3. One trunk contained winter Granddad's skate old photo albums.

_____

_____

4. We unusual found Granddad's old army uniform slice in another trunk.

_____

_____

5. The last trunk was plastic filled with old clothes and books accident.

_____

_____

6. Granddad found a twelve set of old trunk mower keys.

_____

_____

Completing Sentences

A sentence needs a good ending. Read the beginning of each sentence.
Write an ending to complete each sentence. Draw a picture of your
complete sentence.

The kids are planning _____

_____

_____

The travelers stopped at _____

_____

_____

The detective was surprised _____

_____

_____

The artist put a _____

_____

_____

Completing Sentences

A sentence needs a good beginning. Read the ending for each sentence. Write a beginning to complete each sentence. Draw a picture of each sentence.

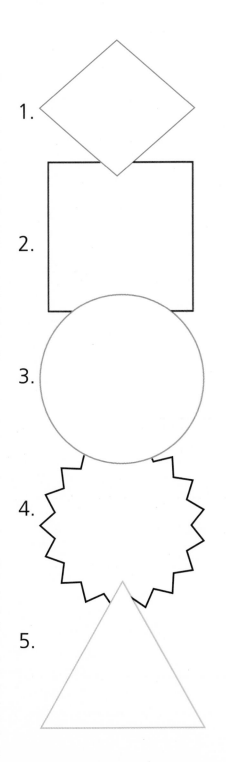

1. _____ at the school picnic tomorrow.

2. _____ so he decided to eat pizza instead.

3. _____ because the doorbell was broken.

4. _____ and put the leaves in the yard bags.

5. _____ if it doesn't rain tomorrow.

Writing Sentences

Look at each word. Write two words that tell something about the picture.
Use the picture name and the two words in a sentence about the picture.

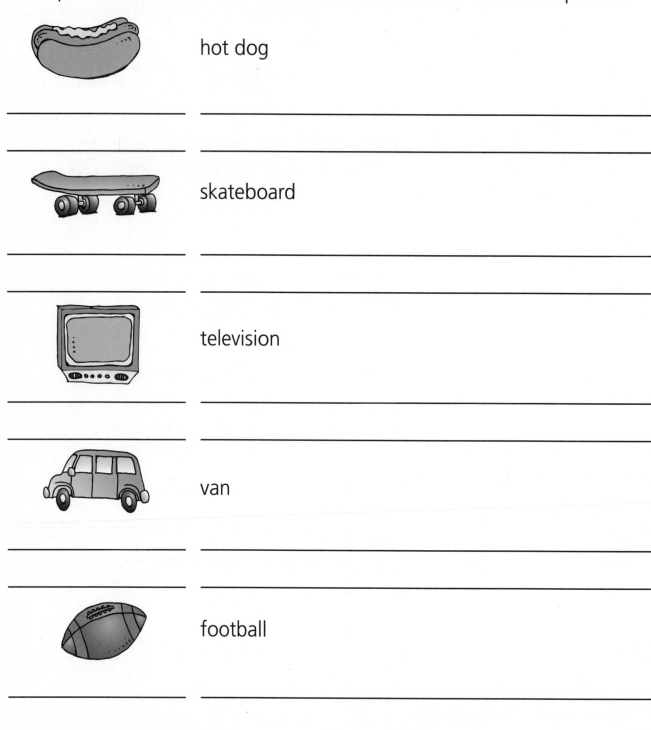

hot dog

_____ _____

_____ _____

skateboard

_____ _____

_____ _____

television

_____ _____

_____ _____

van

_____ _____

_____ _____

football

_____ _____

_____ _____

Statements

- A statement is a sentence that tells something or gives information.

- A statement ends with a period.

Read the sign below. Then read the statements that tell about it.

School Carnival

May 18, 19, 20		5:00 - 8:00 p.m.
Carnival Rides	Hot Dogs	Come one!
Hayride	Balloons	Come all!
Prizes	Games	

Where? school sports field

$1.00	50¢
Adults	Kids

1. The School carnival will start on May 18th at 5:00 p.m.
2. Adults will pay one dollar to get into the carnival.
3. Children will only have to pay fifty cents.
4. The school carnival will be held at the school sports field.
5. There will be carnival rides.

Now read this sign and write five statements to tell about it.

**Warning
Detour Ahead**
Construction on
new bridge
100 feet ahead

Detour will last 3 weeks.
Drive Carefully!
New bridge opens July 4th.

1. _____
_____
2. _____
_____
3. _____
_____
4. _____
_____
5. _____

Statements

A sentence can tell a lot about you. Begin at the START sign and write sentences that tell all about you. Write as many sentences as you can until you reach the center. (Use these questions to help you: How old are you? What color are your eyes? How tall are you? What are your hobbies?)

Questions

- A question is a sentence that asks something.

- A question ends with a question mark.

Read each sentence. Put a question mark (**?**) in the circle at the end of each question.

1. Would you like to go shopping (?)
2. Can we go to the mall (?)
3. How long can you stay (?)
4. I want to go to the department store ◯
5. Where is the book store ◯
6. I am getting hungry ◯
7. Would you like a pizza or a hot dog ◯
8. Do you want another piece of pizza ◯
9. My sister wants me to buy a record for her ◯
10. Where is the escalator ◯
11. The pet store is on the second level ◯
12. Are you going to buy new jeans ◯
13. I want to buy a toy for my little brother ◯

Write three questions that you might ask at a mall.

1. _____

2. _____

3. _____

Questions

Reporters use many questions in their job. Look at each picture. If you were a reporter, what questions would you ask about each picture? Write two questions for each picture.

1._____

2._____

1._____

2._____

1._____

2._____

1._____

2._____

1._____

2._____

1._____

2._____

Exclamations

- An exclamation is a sentence that shows strong feeling or excitement.

- An exclamation ends with an exclamation mark.

The third grade is visiting the museum! Read each sentence. Put an exclamation mark (**!**) at the end of each exclamation.

1. That dinosaur is enor<u>m</u>ous

2. Don't t<u>o</u>uch the mummy

3. The guide i<u>s</u> very helpful

4. This stamp is worth a million d<u>o</u>llars

5. Let's loo<u>k</u> around some more

6. I see the first airpla<u>n</u>e that ever flew

7. He<u>r</u>e is the world's largest diamond

8. We have one more hour to look until <u>l</u>unch

9. Look at the ancient writing <u>o</u>n that wall

10. There is Abraham Lin<u>c</u>oln's coat

11. I want to <u>b</u>uy a guidebook

12. This museum is a great place for <u>k</u>ids

Look What We See

Write the underlined letter from each exclamation to learn what the class sees on its trip to the museum.

____ ____ ____ ____   ____ ____ ____ ____

Exclamations

Look at each picture. Write an exclamation in each speech bubble to tell what the person could be saying.

Commands

- A command is a sentence that tells someone to do something.

- A command ends with a period.

Bob's dad is teaching his brother to drive. Read each sentence. Circle the number of each sentence that is a command.

1. Get in the <u>c</u>ar.

2. Put the k<u>e</u>y in the ignition.

3. Where are your gl<u>a</u>sses?

4. Lock your ca<u>r</u> door.

5. I will open the garage door.

6. Please fasten yo<u>u</u>r safety belt.

7. R<u>e</u>lease the parking brake.

8. I see our neighbor, Mr. O<u>w</u>en.

9. Start the c<u>a</u>r.

10. Watch out <u>f</u>or the pets.

11. Look car<u>e</u>fully around you.

12. Do you see any ot<u>h</u>er cars?

13. <u>B</u>ack out of the driveway.

14. Will you drive carefully down the street?

Write the underlined letter from each circled sentence to see what command Bob gave his brother.

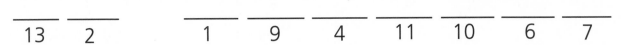

___	___		___	___	___	___	___	___	___
13	2		1	9	4	11	10	6	7

Commands

The kids at Camp Lagoona have not cleaned their cabin. Their leader is telling them what they have to do. Write eight commands that will tell the campers things they must do to clean the cabin.

1. _____

2. _____

3. _____

4. _____

5. _____

6. _____

7. _____

8. _____

Review: Types of Sentences

Read each sentence. Write the correct letter on each line:
S - statement   **Q** - question   **C** - command   **E** - exclamation

_____ My town is fixing up the old theater.

_____ Would the kids at school like to help?

_____ That's a terrific idea!

_____ Tell everyone to be here Saturday morning.

_____ What should we bring?

_____ Bring a ladder and several paintbrushes.

_____ My dad has lots of extra blue paint!

_____ I will ask my teacher to help, too.

_____ We can begin to work when everyone arrives.

_____ Sweep and wax the stage floor.

_____ Put these costumes in the main dressing room.

_____ Look at this old ballet slipper!

_____ I will paint the entrance door black.

_____ Can you repair the torn curtain?

_____ Will you help the other kids clean the seats?

_____ Let's turn on the stage lights.

_____ The old theater is beginning to look great!

_____ Will you be here on opening night?

_____ Our class is planning to sit together.

Review: Types of Sentences

Look at each picture. Write four sentences for each.

S - statement   **Q** - question   **C** - command   **E** - exclamation

S _____

Q _____

C _____

E _____

S _____

Q _____

C _____

E _____

S _____

Q _____

C _____

E _____

S _____

Q _____

C _____

E _____

Writing with Your Senses

Look at the pictures below.

The five **senses** are **seeing**, **hearing**, **smell**, **taste**, and **touch**. Write answers to the following questions about the pictures.

1. What sense are the children in picture A using mainly?

_____

2. What senses are the children in picture B using mainly?

_____

Writing with Your Senses

- You know that details are small parts of a larger whole. You know also that a description is a group of sentences that tells details about something. When you gather details, you use your senses. Sometimes you use just one sense or mainly one sense. Other times, you may use all of your senses.

- Below is a description that uses four of the senses. Read the description. Then write the name of the thing being described.

    It is round and red. It feels smooth. It tastes sweet. It sounds crunchy when you bite it. It is an _____ .

Write On Your Own

Think about a place you like to be. Or you may choose one of the places listed below. Then do the following things: First, write the senses **see**, **hear**, **smell**, **taste**, and **touch** across the top of another sheet of paper. Next, write details that tell about the place you chose under each sense. Finally, write your details together in a complete description. Be sure to write your description in complete sentences.

Ideas

1. your kitchen at holiday time

2. a park in the spring

3. your favorite store

Writing About Feelings

It is starting to rain. Do all the people in the picture feel the same way about the rain? On the lines below, tell how you think they feel and why.

1. The children feel _____

_____

_____

_____

2. The woman feels _____

_____

_____

_____

People can look at the same thing, like rain, differently. The way someone looks at, or views, something is called a point of view. Your point of view may come from where you stand. It may also come from the way you feel.

Writing About Feelings

Sentences can tell about feelings. Read the words in the box. Write three of the words to describe each person. Use the words to write two sentences about the person.

reserved	startled	grumpy
excited	unhappy	shy
shocked	bashful	happy
angry	thrilled	shaken

I feel . . . . 1. _____

_____ _____

_____ 2. _____

_____ _____

I feel . . . . 1. _____

_____ _____

_____ 2. _____

_____ _____

I feel . . . . 1. _____

_____ _____

_____ 2. _____

_____ _____

I feel . . . . 1. _____

_____ _____

_____ 2. _____

_____ _____

Nouns

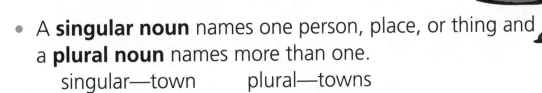

- A **noun** is a word that tells who or what did the action or was acted upon in the sentence.
  The **ringmaster** wore a tall, shiny, black **hat**.

- A **common noun** names any person or place.
  woman   mountain   school

- A **singular noun** names one person, place, or thing and a **plural noun** names more than one.
  singular—town   plural—towns

- A **proper noun** names a particular person or place. Proper nouns start with capital letters.
  Eleanor Roosevelt   Southside School

- A **possessive noun** names who or what owns something.
  Pedro's basketball   the dog's bone   the actor's role

Practice

Circle the common nouns in the following paragraph. Underline the proper nouns.

Dodoes once lived on the island of Mauritius in the Indian Ocean.

Dodoes were very unusual birds. Their wings were very tiny, so dodoes

could not fly. A dodo was as big as a large turkey. These birds no longer

exist.

Nouns
Writing Nouns that are More Exact

1. queen   lion

2. clown   elephant

The person fed the animal.

The sentence above tells about both pictures. But it doesn't tell enough. The nouns person and animal aren't very exact. The next sentence uses more exact nouns to tell about picture 1.

The queen fed the lion.

What more exact nouns would tell about picture 2? Write a sentence with more exact nouns for picture 2 on the line below.

_____

_____

Read the list of nouns below. Then write two nouns that are more exact next to the nouns given. The first one is done for you.

1. building   _____museum_____   _____library_____

2. food   _____   _____

3. toy   _____   _____

Nouns
Writing Nouns that are More Exact

Read the sentences. Look at the nouns. Use more exact nouns to rewrite the sentences to make them more interesting. The first one is done for you.

1. The bird was in the tree.

    <u>The robin was in the oak tree.</u>

2. The animals walked across the land.

    _____

3. The liquid spilled on the floor.

    _____

4. The cookies were in the container.

    _____

5. The flower grew on the bush.

    _____

6. The child played outside.

    _____

7. Someone planted the vegetable.

    _____

8. The person picked out some clothes.

    _____

9. The car went down the street.

    _____

Pronouns

- A **pronoun** is a word that takes the place of a noun or nouns. Pronouns help you avoid using the same nouns over and over. Pronouns change their spelling according to their use.

  John said that **John** was going to ride **John's** bike.

  John said that **he** was going to ride **his** bike.

- **I**, **you**, **she**, and **they** are examples of <u>subject pronouns</u>.

  Squanto was a member of the Pawtuxet tribe.

  He was a member of the Pawtuxet tribe.

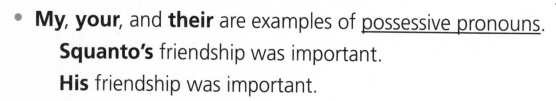

- **Me**, **him**, **us**, and **them** are examples of <u>object pronouns.</u>

  Squanto showed the **colonists** how to fish.

  Squanto showed **them** how to fish.

- **My**, **your**, and **their** are examples of <u>possessive pronouns</u>.

  Squanto's friendship was important.

  His friendship was important.

Practice

Circle the pronouns in the sentences below.

> Have you ever heard of Jane Addams? She wanted to help people living in poverty. There were no government agencies to help them. Addams established a settlement house in Chicago. It was a place to receive help and learn new skills. The settlement house helped many people and made their lives easier.

Proofreading Practice: Pronouns

As you read the story below, you will notice that the pronouns have been used incorrectly. Read the sentences carefully. Circle the incorrect pronouns. Then write the correct pronouns above the words you have circled.

Shopping

Every year Mom and me go shopping together before school starts. It's lots of fun. We leave my brother at home. Him is not happy. Mom and me drive to the shopping mall and plan where to go first. Her wants to do the hard shopping first, so we do. I try on several winter coats, and we decide to buy the purple one with a fur-lined hood. Mom and me pick out gloves and snowpants to match the coat. Then mom and me go to try on jeans and sweaters.

Next, I lead the way into the school supplies store. I see some of my friends. Them are shopping with them moms, too. I pick up two red folders, a big bottle of glue, a box of forty-eight crayons, and twelve markers. Me can use last year's scissors, but I pick out a new bookbag with my favorite cartoon character on it. Mom remembers a ruler and writing paper as I get pencils and a big pink eraser. Mom and me go to the car loaded down with shopping bags.

Adjectives
Writing with Interesting Adjectives

The plane is taking off.

The sentence above tells something about the picture. But it doesn't tell much. It would tell more if it used comparing words. Comparing words tell how things are alike or different. A shorter name for comparing words is adjectives.

Now read the two sentences below that use adjectives to tell more about the picture above. Then underline the adjectives in each sentence.

1. The huge, bright, new plane is taking off.

2. The tiny, clumsy, old plane is taking off.

Underline each adjective in the next group of sentences.

1. Daisy got a shiny, blue bicycle for her birthday.

2. It had a large basket on the handlebars.

3. Last week she took her fluffy kitten for a ride.

4. First, Daisy wrapped the kitten in a soft, green blanket.

Adjectives
Writing About an Object

- Some words always describe things. Words like *smooth, soft*, and *loud* are describing words. You already know a word that means a describing word. That word is *adjective*.

  Look at the picture. Think about the cat. Then circle the adjectives below that describe the cat.

square	fluffy	soft	mad
black	wet	sad	furry

  Now think of two more adjectives that describe the cat. Write those adjectives below.

  1. _____ 2._____

Write On Your Own

On another sheet of paper, write the name of your favorite food, toy, and clothing. Next to each favorite thing, write three adjectives that describe it. Remember to think about your five senses. After you have written your adjectives, choose one of the things to describe. Finally, write four or more sentences that describe your favorite thing. You may use the adjectives below.

Adjectives				
playful	speedy	noisy	cold	tasty
furry	quiet	brown	sharp	sweet
colorful	red	bright	soft	yummy

Adjectives
Writing Better Sentences

• Special words can make a better sentence.

Read each sentence. Write a describing word on each line to make the sentence more interesting. Draw a picture of each sentence.

1. The planet orbits the sun.

   The _____ planet orbits the _____ sun.

2. We collected shells along the beach.

   We collected _____ shells along the _____ beach.

3. The team scored points.

   The _____ team scored _____ points.

4. Six roses were in the vase.

   Six _____ roses were in the _____ vase.

Review: Adjectives and Nouns

A sentence can tell about a specific thing. Write a size word, a color word, and a name of a thing on the lines to complete each sentence. Then draw the missing thing in the pictures below. The first sentence has been done for you.

1. Lisa found a __small__ , __orange__ , __kitten__ by her front door.
   size   color   thing

2. Paul saw a _____, _____, _____ in the water by the boat.
   size   color   thing

3. The winner wore a _____, _____, _____ around his neck.
   size   color   thing

4. A _____, _____, _____ was standing by Pete's sleeping bag.
   size   color   thing

1.

2.

3.

4.

Adverbs

- Adverbs can describe verbs. They tell when, where, or how an action happens.

  The concert will start **soon**. (Soon tells when.)
  The tuba player sits **here**. (Here tells where.)
  The drummer plays **loudly**. (Loudly tells how.)

- Adverbs can describe adjectives. They usually answer the question how or to what degree.

  quite handsome   **too** small   **rather** sweet
  My **really** naughty dog chews **very** old slippers.
  How naughty is my dog? **Really** naughty.
  How old are the slippers? **Very** old.

- Adverbs can also describe other adverbs.

  very quickly   extremely slowly   awfully quietly

Practice

Circle the adverb that describes the verb in bold type. Then circle the question that the adverb answers.

1. The game **started** early in the afternoon.   How?   When?   Where?

2. The Tigers confidently **took** the field.   How?   When?   Where?

3. The batter **walked** slowly to home plate.   How?   When?   Where?

4. The pitcher **threw** there.   How?   When?   Where?

5. The batter easily **hit** the ball.   How?   When?   Where?

6. The crowd **applauded** loudly.   How?   When?   Where?

Adverbs
Writing with More Exact Adverbs

Read the sentence below.

   The snake is crawling **quietly outside now**.

Now write answers to the questions below.

1. Which one of the underlined words tells how the snake is crawling?

   _____

2. Which word tells where the snake is crawling? _____

3. Which word tells when the snake is crawling? _____

Adverbs are words like those underlined above. Adverbs tell **how**, **where**, and **when**. Find the adverbs in the sentences below. Underline each one.

1. I found my slipper outside today.

2. Rags was chewing it happily.

3. I yelled loudly, and he ran.

4. He ran upstairs and hid.

5. Later, I found him sleeping peacefully.

Verbs

- A **verb** is a word that shows action or expresses a state of being. Every sentence must have a verb. A verb such as **Go**! can be a one-word sentence.
    Jump, **shoot**, **listen**, and **read** are action verbs.
    Am, **are**, **is**, **was**, **were**, **be**, **being**, and **been** are all forms of the verb **be**. They tell what someone or something is, was, or will be.

- A **present tense verb** shows action that happens now.
    The farmer **plants** corn in early spring.

- A **past tense verb** shows action that happened earlier.
    The farmer **planted** beans in that field last year.

- A **future tense verb** shows action that will happen.
    Next year, the farmer **will plant** barley.

Practice

Underline the six verbs in the paragraph below. Write a more interesting verb above each verb to make the paragraph more interesting.

Woolly mammoths walked on Earth more than three million years ago. These creatures were about eleven feet tall. They seemed like hairy elephants. Mammoths had moss, grass, and twigs. Early humans killed the woolly mammoth for food and clothing. The last woolly mammoths ended about ten thousand years ago.

Verb Agreement

- The verb has to agree with the subject of the sentence. This means that they must both be either singular or plural.

- Usually if the subject is singular, or the pronoun **he**, **she**, or **it**, add **-s** or **-es** to the verb.

    Dad **remembers** when few homes had TV sets.
    He often **reads** to my little brother.

- If the subject is more than one, or the pronoun **I**, **you**, **we**, or **they**, do <u>not</u> add **-s** or **-es** to the verb.

    My parents always **watch** the news on TV.
    I **ride** my bike to school.

Practice

Write the verb on the line that correctly completes each sentence.

1. Adam ___works___ on the new computer. (works, work)

2. He ___uses___ it to do his homework. (use, uses)

3. His brothers ___play___ games on it. (plays, play)

4. His mom ___writes___ stories on it. (writes, write)

5. His sister ___types___ reports for school. (type, types)

6. Computers ___make___ many jobs easier. (makes, make)

Regular Verb Tense

- **Tense** is a word that means "time." The tense of a verb tells you when the action takes place.

- A verb in the **present tense** shows action that happens now.
   The soccer players **kick** the ball toward the net.

- A verb in the **past tense** shows action that already happened. Add **-ed** to form the past tense of most verbs.
   The soccer players **kicked** the ball toward the net.

- To form the past tense of verbs that end in **e**, drop the **e** and add **-ed**.
   rake—rak**ed**   place—plac**ed**   taste—tast**ed**

Practice

Write the past tense of the verb in parentheses.

1. We _____ to the movies. (walk)

2. We didn't know that Len's dog _____ us. (follow)

3. We didn't notice that people _____ at us. (point)

4. We finally _____ around. (turn)

5. Skipper _____ a dollar bill in his mouth. (carry)

Irregular Verb Tense

- Some verbs are special. They do not end in **-ed** to show past time. These verbs are called **irregular verbs** because they do not follow the pattern for forming the past tense. They have one special spelling to show past time.

     Erica **takes** us to the city each month. (present)
     Last month, she **took** us to the art museum. (past)
     We usually **ride** the train to the city. (present)
     On our last trip, we **rode** the bus. (past)

- Other irregular verbs include:

break—broke	begin—began	
come—came	do—did	draw—drew
eat—ate	make—made	think—thought
write—wrote	say—said	catch—caught
run—ran	grow—grew	win—won
give—gave	spring—sprung	buy—bought

Practice

Write the past tense of the verb over each underlined irregular verb in the sentences below.

Julio <u>run</u> in a 5K race last week. He <u>think</u> that he would win. Tanya <u>come</u> from behind and <u>catch</u> up with Julio. Tanya passed him and <u>win</u> the race. She <u>break</u> the school record. Julio <u>do</u> not feel bad about losing the race. He <u>say</u> he will try harder next time.

Verbs
Writing with Interesting Verbs

The canoe **tipped**, and the boy **fell** into the water.

The words that are underlined in the sentence above are called verbs. Verbs tell action or help make a statement in other ways. If you choose exact verbs, they will help you say just what you want to say.

Read the sentences below. Then underline each verb.

1. Jan danced on the stage.

2. A frog jumped into my soup.

3. The squirrel scurried up the tree.

The most exact verbs make the most interesting sentences. Read the list of verbs below. Then write two verbs that are more exact next to the verbs given. The first one is done to show you how.

1. ran   _____sprinted_____   _____raced_____

2. walked   _____   _____

3. ate   _____   _____

4. talked   _____   _____

Writing with Interesting Verbs

Look at the picture below. There is lots of action. On the lines below, tell what is happening in the picture. Use exact verbs to make your sentences interesting.

_____

_____

_____

_____

_____

_____

_____

_____

Comparisons

- **Adjectives** are words that describe nouns.

- The ending **-er** is added to most adjectives that compare two people, places, or things. The ending **-est** is added to most adjectives to compare more than two people, places, or things.
    A coyote can run **faster** than a bear.
    The cheetah is the **fastest** animal of all.

- If the adjective ends with an **e**, drop the **e** before adding the **-er** or **-est** ending.
    large   larg**er**   larg**est**

- If the adjective ends with a single vowel and a consonant, double the consonant and add the **-er** or **-est** ending.
    big   bigg**er**   bigg**est**

- If the adjective ends with a consonant and **y**, change the **y** to **i** before adding **-er** or **-est**.
    tiny   tin**ier**   tin**iest**

- Some long adjectives use **more** and **most**.
    beautiful   **more** beautiful   **most** beautiful

Practice

Write the correct adjective on each line.

1. We just had the _____ summer in history. (hotter, hottest)

2. Dad was _____ about the weather than we were. (happier, happiest)

3. His roses were _____ than ever. (more beautiful, most beautiful)

Comparisons of Pictures

- When we compare things, we tell how they are alike or how they are different. The sentences beside the pictures are comparisons.

  Study the pictures. Then read the comparisons. Finally, underline the comparisons that best tell about the pictures.

1.     One player is taller.

   One player is thinner.

2.     One animal is longer.

   One animal is smarter.

3.     The boy and girl are the same height.

   The boy is in the fifth grade.

Write On Your Own

On another sheet of paper, draw two sets of pictures. Draw the pictures in each set so that you can write comparisons for them. Then write a comparison for each set. Be sure to write your comparisons in complete sentences. You can use these words to get you started.

Words Used in Comparisons

more	fewer	louder	less
faster	same	bigger	higher

Comparisons Using <u>er</u> and <u>more</u>

Miff   Thor

Miff is <u>smaller</u> than Thor.   Thor is <u>larger</u> than Miff.

Both sentences above are comparisons. You already know that comparisons tell how things are alike or different. Some comparing words add **er** to their ends to make comparisons.

small—small**er**   tall—tall**er**   high—high**er**

Now read the next sentence.

A feather bed is **more comfortable** than a bed of nails.

What are the words that make the comparison in this sentence? Words like comfortable use the word **more** to make comparisons. Most long words use the word **more** to make certain comparisons.

beautiful—more beautiful   important—more important
dangerous—more dangerous

Using the list of comparing words, write two comparisons for the picture below. Add **er** to the correct words. Use **more** with longer words.

small   fancy   new

long   short

comfortable

beautiful

_____

_____

Comparisons Using est and most

- Read the following paragraph.

   Flora is the clever**est** magician I know. She can do the **most** wonderful tricks. Her new**est** trick is to make herself disappear. Too bad she hasn't learned how to make herself appear again!

Cleverest, **newest**, and **most wonderful** are all forms of comparisons. They compare more than two things. When comparing more than two things, add **est** to the ends of short comparing words. But use the word **most** before longer comparing words.

Read the following comparing words. Write the word **two** beside those that can compare two things. Write the words **more than two** beside those that can compare more than two things.

1. greatest _____

2. greater _____

3. most wonderful _____

Write a comparison sentence for each comparing word below. Write each comparison so that it compares more than two things. The two forms are done to show you how.

thoughtful <u>Harry is the most thoughtful person I know.</u>

great <u>That was the greatest time of my life.</u>

1. old _____

2. delicious _____

3. tall _____

Comparisons
Review

- Some comparing words drop, add, or change letters when they change form. For example: funny, funn**ier**, funn**iest** — large, larg**er**, larg**est**. If you are not sure of the spelling, check your dictionary.

Write three comparisons for the picture below. You may use the following comparing words or think up your own: large, big, small, little. Be sure to check your spelling.

1. _____

2. _____

3. _____

Write On Your Own

Pretend you are the judge at a costume party. You have to choose the funniest costume, the ugliest costume, and the most unusual costume. On a separate sheet of paper, write five or more sentences that will tell about the costumes. Be sure to use the correct form for each comparison you write.

Comparisons Using <u>like</u> and <u>as</u>

- Look at the picture. Then read the sentences below that tell about it.

My horse runs **like the wind**.
My horse runs **as fast as the wind**.

- Another way to compare things is to use the words **like** or **as**. When used in comparisons, the words **like** and **as** tell how things compare. This type of comparison is also known as a **simile**.

Read the sentences about the picture again. Then answer the following questions.

1. To what are the sentences comparing the way the horse runs?

_____

2. How many things are being compared in the first sentence?

_____

3. How many things are being compared in the second sentence?

_____

Read the following comparisons. Then write your own comparisons by finishing the phrases below.

> Daria's smile is like a slice of watermelon.
> She is as thin as a wrinkle.

1. Chico laughs like _____

2. Our car is like _____

3. The pudding looks like _____

Writing Similes

A sentence can use fun expressions. Read each sentence. Write a word on each line to complete the sentence. Draw a picture of each sentence.

1. The _____ is as

   slow as a _____ .

2. My _____ is as

   quick as a _____ .

Read each sentence. Finish the sentences with interesting comparisons. The first two are done for you.

1. She worked ____ like a horse. _____

2. She had eyes ____ like twinkling stars. _____

3. The tree was as straight as _____

4. The snow was as cold as _____

5. The water is as warm as _____

6. The boy was as strong as _____

7. He played basketball like _____

8. The sun was as hot as _____

Spectrum Writing Grade 3

Comparisons Using <u>good</u> and <u>bad</u>

Read the sentences below that tell about the picture.

Sam has a **good** seat.
Felicia has a **better** seat than Sam.
Yolanda has the **best** seat of the three.

Now read these sentences.
Marybeth's bike is in **bad** shape.
Nazir's bike is in **worse** shape than Marybeth's.
Frank's bike is in the **worst** shape of the three.

Read the sentences above again. Then answer the following questions. Write your answers on the lines.

1. What word compares two seats? _____

2. What word compares more than two seats? _____

3. What word compares two bikes? _____

4. What word compares more than two bikes? _____

Comparisons Using <u>good</u> and <u>bad</u>

Using the two forms of good and bad that you have learned, write your own comparisons on the lines below. The examples below will show you how.

Good

good	John is a **good** singer.
better	Manny is a **better** singer than John.
best	Estella is the **best** singer of the three.

Bad

bad	Angela has a **bad** cold.
worse	Glen has a **worse** cold than Angela.
worst	Melinda has the **worst** cold of the three.

1. good _____

2. better _____

3. best _____

4. bad _____

5. worse_____

6. worst _____

Write On Your Own

On another sheet of paper, write about something you saw or something that happened to you. Using a comparison of **good** or **bad,** write at least five sentences. You may use the ideas below or you may think up your own.

The Best Summer Vacation   The Worst Storm

Polishing Your Writing

Two people went there. They saw some funny things. They enjoyed it very much.

The story above doesn't tell very much. But you can make it more interesting when you rewrite it. You can use exact nouns and verbs. You can add adjectives to describe people and things. You can add adverbs to tell where, when, or how. You can check to see that all verbs tell about the same time.

Now rewrite the story at the top of the page. Make it as interesting as you can.

_____

_____

_____

_____

_____

_____

_____

_____

_____

Writing About a Person

• You know some words that describe objects. There are words that describe people, too.

Write the word or word group from the list under the picture of the person it describes. Some words may not fit either person.

Words That Can Describe People

tall	curly hair	wearing glasses
short	long hair	flowered dress
thin	dark hair	light hair
freckles	short hair	long pants

_____   _____

_____   _____

_____   _____

_____   _____

Writing About a Person

Write four or more sentences that describe the picture above. Try to describe everything that the picture shows. Tell how the boy looks, how he is dressed, and how he feels.

_____

_____

_____

_____

Write On Your Own

Think about one of your favorite people. Think about how that person looks and how he or she acts. Think about what that person does best. Think about why you like that person. Then, on another sheet of paper, write five sentences that describe your favorite person. Remember to use exact nouns, verbs, and adjectives.

The Writing Process

- The **Writing Process** is a set of steps to help you make your writing the best it can be. Read about the **Writing Process** below. You'll get to try each step on your own in the pages that follow.

1 Prewriting

Prewriting is what you do before you write. It is a way of collecting your thoughts and ideas for what you want to write about. Sometimes it is called **brainstorming**.

2 Drafting

Your first try at a piece of writing is called a **rough draft**. When you write a rough draft, don't worry about spelling and punctuation. Just get your writing started!

3 Revising

Revising means to make corrections. When you revise your writing, you want to be sure it makes sense. You want to make sure nothing is missing. This is also a good time to check that you have used interesting words.

4 Proofreading

When you **proofread** your writing, you are looking for mistakes. Now, it is time to check your spelling, punctuation, and to make sure you capitalized words correctly.

5 Publishing

When you **publish** your writing, you are ready for people to read it! You should use your best handwriting and a nice clean piece of paper. Or, you can type your piece of writing on a computer.

Prewriting

- The first step of the writing process is called **prewriting**. **Pre-** means "before," so **prewriting** means "before writing." This is the time when you get to **think** about writing. Here are some questions you can ask yourself when you are **prewriting**:

What do I want to write about?
What do I know a lot about?
Where can I find information?
What are some words or ideas I can use for my topic?

Now let's practice doing some prewriting!

A topic for writing is **animals**. Can you answer these prewriting questions about **animals**? Write down whatever you think of.

What animals do I want to write about? _____

_____

What animal do I know a lot about? _____

_____

What are some words or ideas about that animal? _____

_____

Where can I find more information about that animal?_____

_____

Prewriting

Brainstorming helps you organize your ideas. Read each question. Write your ideas on the lines. Use your ideas to write five sentences about some of your favorite sports.

What are some popular sports?

1. _____   3. _____   5. _____
2. _____   4. _____

What equipment is used?

1. _____   3. _____   5. _____
2. _____   4. _____

Where are these sports played?

1. _____   3. _____   5. _____
2. _____   4. _____

Sports Fun

1. _____
2. _____
3. _____
4. _____
5. _____

Prewriting

- Another prewriting method is **writing webs**, also called story webs or clustering. Again, you think of everything you can about a topic. Then you write each idea down like this:

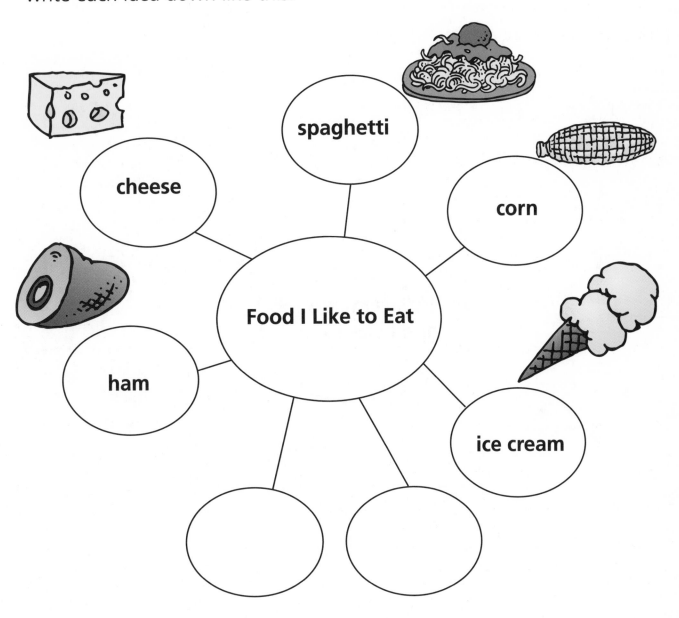

Can you add two more ideas to this web?

Prewriting

Here is another topic for you. Can you fill in the web with words and ideas that you could write about?

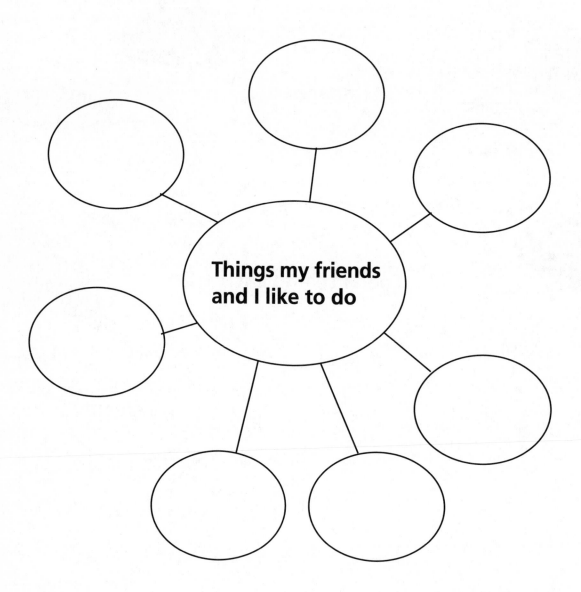

Things my friends and I like to do

Prewriting

• Another kind of prewriting is called **freewriting**. It is just what it sounds like. You are free to write whatever comes to mind. You just start writing and keep going. Don't worry about what fits. Don't worry about spelling, capitalization, or punctuation. You can fix that later.

Freewriting lets your ideas come out! **Just write!**

Here is an example of freewriting.

I just wanted to help. It was a hot day. Mom came in with lots of groceries. Shee needed help. I wanted to show her I was responsable. I got lots of stuff out of the bags. Some fell on the floor. I like cookies. Mom was happy.

Can you figure out what the topic was?

_____

Drafting

- Step Two of the writing process is called **drafting**. It is time to take all of the ideas and words you came up with during prewriting and begin to write the real thing.

Choose one of your topics from any of the Prewriting pages. Write your ideas on the lines below. You may even have new ideas that you can add here. Remember, your prewriting only needs to be words or short phrases. You'll write complete sentences later when you practice drafting.

_____

_____

_____

_____

Using the ideas above, draw a picture of your topic.

Drafting

Now it is time to practice **drafting**. Look at all of the ideas you have about your topic from page 76. Which ones go together?

Take the ideas and words and make complete sentences.

Example: (ideas)   cows, chickens, horses, goats

On the farm I see lots of animals. There are cows, chickens, horses, and goats.

Now write some sentences using your ideas from page 76.

_____

_____

_____

_____

_____

_____

_____

_____

_____

_____

Rough Draft

All of the sentences you drafted on page 77 can be put in order to make a story. Can you put your sentences together so your story makes sense? Try it on the lines below:

_____

_____

_____

_____

_____

_____

_____

_____

_____

_____

_____

Revising

- After drafting, it is time for step three of the writing process, **revising**. To **revise** means "to change."

Look closely at what you have written. You want to ask yourself questions like:

Does this make sense?
Have I used describing words (nouns, verbs, adjectives)?
Am I missing anything?
Does everything fit here?
Should I take something out?
Do I have things in a good order?

Then you **revise** the sentences until you have a better story. Don't worry about spelling, capitalization, or punctuation yet. That will come next.

Look at the sentences below. Revise each one to make it a more interesting sentence. Then draw a line to the number to show which sentence should come first, second, and third.

1 After school, Jon did something.

_____

2 At bedtime, he read something.

_____

3 In the morning, Jon ate something.

_____

Just So You Know

Sometimes you will revise more than once before a sentence or story is really terrific.

Revising

Remember: When you **revise**, ask yourself these questions:

Does this make sense?
Have I used describing words (nouns, verbs, adjectives)?
Am I missing anything?
Does everything fit here?
Should I take something out?
Do I have things in a good order?

Look at the story you wrote on page 78. **Revise** it on the lines below.

_____

_____

_____

_____

_____

_____

_____

_____

How does your story look now? Do you like it better?
Show your story to a parent or friend. Does he or she have any ideas to help you revise your story even more?

Proofreading

How do you like your story now? If you need to revise it more, use another sheet of paper.

When you are done **revising**, it is time for Step Four of the writing process, **proofreading**.

Now you can fix mistakes in

spelling
capitalization
punctuation

Here are some **proofreading marks** that will help you. See how they are used in the story below.

I went to schoool yesterday. I forgot my books.They were at home. Why did I forget them? My dog, scotty, was sleeping on then. miss jones didn't scold me. She was really nice to mee. Maybe Miss Jones has a dog at her house to.

Proofreading Marks

misspelling: ⬭

capitalize: ☰ ohio

add . . .

a period: ⊙

an apostrophe: ⱽ

Proofreading

It's time to practice proofreading. Remember: You are looking for mistakes in:

spelling	I ate (for) eggs. *four*
punctuation	Wait! You can't go there⊙
capitalization	scott caught a Fish in the lake.

The **proofreading marks** are here to help you.

Proofreading Marks

misspelling:	⬭
capitalize:	≡ ohio
lowercase	/ Sister

add . . .

a period:	⊙
an apostrophe:	⋁
a question mark:	?
an exclamation point:	!

It s lunch time! We have fun eeting our lunch with louis. he does magick tricks for us Look at how he makes my spoon disappear Can he make it come back I hope so. I want to eat my pudding.

Proofread these sentences, too.

The clintonville cubs have a game on tusday.

Who are they playing I want too go watch tham.

I ll go, to. Pick me up at twevle o'clock

Proofreading

The more you practice proofreading the better your writing will be. Practice proofreading the sentences below. Write the corrected sentences on the lines.

I saw a huge moose wen we went camping

_____

_____

Did you mak a wish at the the wishing Well

_____

_____

the playground is a Fun place for freinds.

_____

_____

The Baby needs a botle of milk rite away!

_____

_____

It s time for bed. Will you read me a storie

_____

_____

_____

Proofreading Marks	**add . . .**
misspelling: ⬭	a comma: ∧
capitalize: ☰ ohio	an apostrophe: ∨
lowercase: / Sister	a period: ⊙
	a question mark: ?

Publishing

- Step Five of the writing process is called **publishing**.
  There are lots of ways to **publish** your writing. Look at the examples below.

How would you publish your writing?

_____

_____

_____

_____

Proofreading and Publishing

Now go back to your story on page 80. Look at what you wrote. Proofread your story for mistakes.

Now write the final draft on the lines below.

_____

_____

_____

_____

_____

_____

_____

_____

_____

_____

_____

_____

Now your writing is all done. You have fixed all of the mistakes. You have written or typed your writing neatly. It is ready for others to read. Show your story to a parent or friend. When you have done all these things, you have **published** your writing!

Writing the Main Idea of a Picture

Look at the picture. What is the picture about?

A picture can tell us many things. But most pictures tell us one **main idea**. The main idea is what the picture is all about. The main idea is what the whole picture means.

Which sentence below tells the main idea of the whole picture above? Circle your answer.

1. Some girls and boys are playing volleyball.

2. Some girls have curly hair.

3. Some boys are playing volleyball.

Which sentence below tells the main idea of this picture?

1. Fred has a new job.

2. Fred's apron is white.

3. Fred is cooking hamburgers.

Writing the Main Idea of a Picture

Draw a picture in the space below. Then write the main idea of your picture on the line.

The main idea of my picture is: _____

_____

Write On Your Own

On another sheet of paper, draw three more pictures. Then under each picture, write its main idea. You might want to use the ideas below. Or think up your own ideas for the pictures.

Ideas
Something that happens at school
Something that happens at home
Something that happens at play

Writing a Title

Look at the picture below.

A **title** is a name for a picture or story. It tells what the picture or story is all about. A title is a short way to tell the main idea of a picture or story.

Look at the picture again. Then read the titles below. Circle the title that best tells about the picture.

1. Sunny Day at the Park

2. Playing in the Park

3. Some People Don't Ride Bicycles

Writing a Title

Read this story.

First, Charlotte hit her toe when she jumped out of bed. Then she had no clean socks to wear. At breakfast she burned her toast. Then she spilled her juice on her homework. It was not a good beginning to Charlotte's day.

What title below best tells about the whole story? Circle your answer.

1. Charlotte's Day

2. The Burned Toast

3. A Bad Beginning for Charlotte

Read the next story. Think about its main idea. Then write a title for the story on the line below.

Have you ever seen a UFO? Some people think UFOs fly around. But nobody knows what they are. Nobody knows if they are real. Some people say they have seen UFOs. Other people say UFOs are a trick.

A good title for this story is:_____

Write On Your Own

On a separate sheet of paper, write your own story. Make it four or more sentences long. Then write a title for your story on the top line of your paper. You can use one of the ideas below. Or you can think up your own idea.

Man Wins Pancake Flipping Contest
Girl Invents New Glue
Elephant Escapes from Zoo

Writing Story Parts in Order

- Some stories are true. For example, most news stories are true. Most stories about real people's lives are true. Can you think of a story about a real person that is true?

- Some stories are not true. They are about what a writer has imagined. They are make-believe. For example, *Cinderella* is a make-believe story. Can you think of another make-believe story?

- Whether stories are true or make-believe, they all have a **beginning**, a **middle**, and an **end**. The beginning, middle, and end of a story are written in sequence. The beginning comes first, the middle comes second, and the ending comes last.

Read each story below. Then write **beginning**, **middle**, or **end** beside the correct part.

1. _____Vera picked up a large egg.

    _____A baby bird hopped out of the egg.

    _____She broke it.

2. _____Next, a snake came out of the man's basket.

    _____First, the man began to play his horn.

    _____Finally, the snake began to sway to the music.

Writing Story Parts in Order

Each group of sentences below can tell a story. But one part of each story is not finished. Write the beginning, middle, or end of each story. Then write the word **beginning**, **middle** or **end** beside the part you have written.

1. It began to snow in the early evening.
   It snowed all night.

   In the morning _____

   _____

2. Jamie and I built a large boat.

   We _____

   _____

   Then we landed on a small island with strange animals.

3. The mailman _____

   _____

   I opened the package as quickly as I could.
   I found a sweater with my name on it.

Write On Your Own

On another sheet of paper, write a story that tells about the funniest thing that ever happened to you. Be sure your story has a beginning, a middle, and an end. Your story can be make-believe or true.

Story Sequence

A story needs a good ending. Look at the beginning and middle of this boy's dream. Write three sentences to tell what happened at the end. Draw a picture. Then write three sentences to tell what is happening at the beginning and in the middle.

Beginning

1. _____

_____

2. _____

_____

3. _____

_____

Middle

1. _____

_____

2. _____

_____

3. _____

_____

End

1. _____

_____

2. _____

_____

Writing the Main Idea of a Paragraph

Read the paragraph below.

Fish sleep in different ways. Some sleep in the sand. Some sleep on their sides. Others sleep on their tails. One fish sleeps while standing on its head!

You know that pictures have main ideas. Well, paragraphs have main ideas, too. The main idea of a paragraph is what the paragraph is all about.

Read the paragraph about fish again. Then circle the sentence below that tells its main idea.

1. Fish are lazy.

2. Fish sleep differently.

3. Some fish sleep in the sand.

Read the next paragraph.

I got up early. I jumped out of bed. Quickly, I washed and dressed. Then I ran down the stairs. I gulped down my breakfast. I couldn't wait to go on my first camping trip.

What is the main idea of the paragraph? Circle the best answer.

1. I rushed to go camping.

2. I ate a big breakfast.

3. I ran down the stairs.

Writing the Main Idea of a Paragraph

Write your own paragraph on the lines below. Make your paragraph at least four sentences long. You can choose one of the ideas below. Or you can think up your own idea.

I love to go skiing.
One day, I got lost while shopping.

_____

_____

_____

_____

No write a sentence on the lien below that tells the main i dea of your paragraph.

_____

Write On Your Own

On another sheet of paper, write two paragraphs. Write one paragraph about something that truly happened. Write the other paragraph about something you can imagine might happen. Write "I imagine" above the make-believe paragraph. Write "This really happened" above the paragraph that is true. Then write the main idea of each paragraph below it. Here are some ideas you may want to use. Or you can think up your own ideas.

The last day of school   Building a tree house
The day I went sky diving   Finding a million dollars

Writing Paragraphs that Make Sense

What doesn't make sense in this picture?

Did you ever read something that didn't make sense? Something that doesn't make sense can juggle your mind. It can mix you up. A picture should make sense. A paragraph should make sense, too. A paragraph makes sense if all its sentences tell about the main idea.

Read the next paragraph. Think about the main idea as you read.

   Tulips are my favorite flowers. I love to see the red, yellow, pink, and orange flowers in rows. Tulips tell me that spring is here. We have to stand in rows at school.

Answer the following questions about the paragraph. Write your answers on the lines.

1. What is the main idea of the paragraph? _____

_____

2. Which sentence doesn't make sense in the paragraph? _____

_____

3. Why doesn't one sentence make sense in the paragraph? _____

_____

Writing Paragraphs that Make Sense

Read the next two paragraphs. Then write your answers on the lines below each one.

> Our neighbor told us about her trip to Europe. She traveled by boat. One night, she met a prince. She married him. I took a trip to Disney World. Then she decided she missed home too much. She flew on the fastest plane. She arrived home yesterday.

1. The main idea is: _____

_____

2. The sentence that doesn't make sense in the paragraph is: _____

_____

> Tugboats are small boats used to move large ships. I'd like to sail a ship someday. A tugboat's engine is very powerful. The small boat can pull or push. It's fun to see tugboats moving big ships around.

3. The main idea is: _____

_____

4. The sentence that doesn't make sense in the paragraph is: _____

_____

Write On Your Own

Use this main idea: "One day I put my shoes on the wrong feet." Or use your own main idea. Then, on a separate sheet of paper, write a paragraph using the main idea you have chosen. Remember: Use only sentences that belong with the main idea.

Writing Paragraphs that Make Sense

- You know that a paragraph is a group of sentences about one subject. Read the sentences in the paragraph. Put a line under the sentences that do not belong. Then write the correct sentences to make a paragraph.

Yesterday I tried out for the All-School Swim Team. I got up early to exercise and eat a good breakfast. The sweater was too big. Everyone met at the pool at 10:00 A.M. I finished my homework. The coach had us swim laps to warm up.

My sister's birthday is tomorrow. He divided us into small groups. Each group swam four strokes for him. I lost my new skateboard. The coach watched carefully and then made notes. Tomorrow he will announce the new team.

_____

_____

_____

_____

_____

_____

_____

Writing Paragraphs that Make Sense

The main idea of a paragraph is also known as the topic sentence. You have practiced writing the main idea of a paragraph and learned that sentences in a paragraph make sense. Here is some more practice for you. Read each topic sentence. Write a paragraph about the subject in each topic sentence.

This morning my mom took me to shop for new clothes for school.

_____

_____

_____

_____

_____

_____

Yesterday I got my first pair of glasses.

_____

_____

_____

_____

_____

_____

Writing Paragraphs that Make Sense

Look at the picture. Write a topic sentence. Write other sentences to make a paragraph to tell about the picture.

_____

_____

_____

_____

_____

_____

_____

Proofreading Practice:
Writing Paragraphs that Make Sense

As you read the article below, you will notice sentences that do not belong. Read the sentences carefully. Circle the sentences that do not belong in the story.

The Changing Seasons

It takes the earth one year to go around the sun one time. Don't you wish the earth would move faster? The earth doesn't point straight up and down. The earth tilts a little to one side. The earth tilts on a pretend stick that goes through the earth from pole to pole. We call this "stick" the axis. It's because of the earth's tilt on its axis that we have different seasons. The tilt does not change as the earth circles the sun.

When the part of the earth you live on tilts toward the sun, you get more daylight hours and more direct heat from the sun. This would be the summer season. I think summer is the best season because you can go swimming. When your part of the earth begins to tilt away from the sun, you start to get less sunlight and less heat. We call this season fall. Fall is when football is played. You also have to rake the fallen leaves.

When the tilt of the earth is farthest away from the sun, you get the fewest daylight hours and heat from the sun. This is winter. Winter is fun when it snows.

When the earth's tilt once again begins to get closer to the sun, we get more heat and daylight hours. This is the season we call spring.

Writing Picture Stories

Look at the groups of pictures below. They can tell a story. Put each group of pictures in correct order so that they do tell a story. Write **first**, **next** or **last** under each picture to show the correct order.

_____first_____   _____   _____

_____   _____   _____

When you put each group of pictures above in order, you put them in **sequence**. Sequence tells you what comes first, next, or last.

Writing Picture Stories

The pictures below are in sequence. They tell part of a story.
Finish the story by drawing the last picture in the space.

First

Next

Last

On each line below, write a sentence that tells about each picture above. Be sure that your sentences are in sequence.

First: _____

Next: _____

Last: _____

Write On Your Own

On another sheet of paper, draw your own picture story. Use at least three pictures for your story. Then write a sentence under each picture that tells about the picture. Be sure your pictures and sentences are in sequence. You can use the ideas below. Or you can think up your own idea.

Planning a Friend's Birthday Party
Practicing a Music Lesson
Feeding Your Baby Sister

Writing Sequence Words

Study the pictures above. The words that are underlined are **sequence** words. Sequence words tell when something happens. *First*, *then*, *next*, and *finally* are sequence words. Some other sequence words are *last*, *second*, *third*, *tomorrow*, *yesterday*, *before*, and *after*.

Read the lists of sequence words below. Then number each word to show which word tells first, second, or last. Use the numbers 1, 2, or 3.

___ middle   ___ night

___ beginning   ___ morning

___ end   ___ noon

Find the sequence words in the next paragraph. Circle each one.

   First, I gave the crazy monkey a banana. Then she peeled it. Finally, she threw away the banana and ate the peel.

Proofreading Practice
Writing Sequence Words

As you read the story below, you will find that sequence words have been left out. Use clue words like **first**, **next**, **then**, and **finally** to show the sequence in the story.

Teacher for the Day

If I were a teacher for the day, this is what I would do. I would put a basket of candy and gum just inside the door and let the students take as much as they wanted when they arrived.

I would let everyone pick a seat beside a friend. We would go outside to recess and play games.

We would go on a field trip to a circus. After the field trip, we would eat cookies and ice cream.

It would be time to go home. I would let the students take more candy out of the basket as they left the room. My students would tell me that they hoped I would be their teacher tomorrow.

Combining Sentences

To combine sentences that have some of the words repeated, use the repeated words only once and the word **and** to join the sentences. Remember to change the verb form to agree with the plural subject.

Maria likes to hike in the mountains.
Tanya likes to hike in the mountains.
Maria and Tanya like to hike in the mountains.

If you use **I** as part of a combined subject, do not forget to put **I** last.

I am going to summer camp.
Keith is going to summer camp.
Keith and I are going to summer camp.

Practice

Combine each set of sentences below to form one sentence. Use **and** to connect two nouns or pronouns.

1. My grandpa collects stamps. I collect stamps.

   _____

2. My sister sometimes gives me stamps. My dad sometimes gives me stamps.

   _____

3. Rare stamps are valuable. Stamps with printing errors are valuable.

   _____

Combining Sentences

- A good writer can combine sentences in several ways. One way is to combine two sentences that have some of the words repeated. Use the repeated words only once, and use **and** or **or** to join the sentences.

Gloria washed the dishes. Gloria dried the dishes.
Gloria washed **and** dried the dishes.

Gloria could dust the furniture. Gloria could vacuum the carpet.
Gloria could dust the furniture **or** vacuum the carpet.

Practice

Combine each pair of sentences below into one sentence that has two verbs, or action words.

1. Helen Keller could not see. Helen Keller could not hear.

   _____

2. Helen could read Braille. Helen could write on a special typewriter.

   _____

3. She went to high school. She graduated from Radcliffe College.

   _____

4. Helen wrote books. Helen received many honors for helping others.

   _____

Combining Sentences

- A good writer can combine sentences in several ways. One way is to use **and** to combine sentences that have some of the words repeated so that the repeated words are used only once.

    Kenji likes apples. Kenji likes oranges.
    Kenji likes apples **and** oranges.

If more than two things are named, put a comma after each one, and add **and** before the last one.

    Veronica has a dog. Veronica has a cat. Veronica has two goldfish.
    Veronica has a dog, a cat, **and** two goldfish.

Practice

Combine each set of sentences below into one sentence.

1. Our class took a trip to New York City. Our class took a trip to Washington, D.C.

   _____

2. We traveled by plane. We traveled by train. We traveled by bus.

   _____

3. We saw the Empire State Building. We saw the World Trade Center. We saw the Washington Monument.

   _____

   _____

Combining Sentences

- Sometimes you can improve your writing by using one or two words in place of a whole sentence.

    Grandma baked muffins.
    They were delicious.
    Grandma baked **delicious** muffins.

- You can often combine basic information from several sentences into one sentence.

    Grandma has a garden. It is in the backyard. It is big.
    Grandma has a **big** garden **in the backyard** or
    Grandma has a **big, backyard** garden.

Practice

Combine each group of sentences below into one sentence.

1. Rosa is going on a trip. She is going to Dallas. The trip is short.

   _____

2. She packs a suitcase. It is brown. It is big.

   _____

3. Uncle Larry carries the suitcase to the car. The suitcase is heavy.

   _____

4. Doug meets Rosa at the airport. Rosa is Doug's cousin.

   _____

Combining Sentences

- In writing, you can combine short sentences to save space and add variety. Sometimes you can improve your writing by using a phrase in place of a whole sentence.

  My birthday present was a CD player. It was from Mom and Dad.
  My birthday present from Mom and Dad was a CD player.

Practice

Combine each pair of sentences into one sentence. Use a phrase in place of one sentence.

1. Oscar went sailing. He went with Ramon.

   _____

2. They sailed east. They left from the harbor.

   _____

3. Oscar had supplies. He stored them beneath the deck.

   _____

4. They docked the boat. The dock was past the cove.

   _____

5. Oscar and Ramon had a picnic. They sat near some rocks.

   _____

Combining Sentences

Read the two sentences. Choose the important word or words from the second sentence to add to the first sentence where the ↓ is.

1. I have a new ↓ skateboard.
   It is purple and black.

   _____

   _____

2. I am writing a ↓ letter to my cousin.
   It is a thank-you letter.

   _____

3. We ate ↓ after the homecoming game.
   We ate hot dogs and chili.

   _____

4. I have to study for my ↓ test.
   My test is in science.

   _____

5. My sister is playing ↓ in the concert.
   She is playing the cello.

   _____

Sentence Building

A sentence can tell more and more. Read the sentences. Look at the underlined word or words. On the lines, write **who**, **what**, **where**, or **when** to tell what the words tell in the sentence.

On the lines, combine the sentences into one sentence.

_____ The magician did <u>tricks</u>.

_____ The magician did tricks <u>for the kids</u>.

_____ The magician did tricks <u>at the show</u>.

_____ The magician did tricks <u>yesterday</u>.

_____

_____

_____ I ate cake <u>and ice cream</u>.

_____ I ate cake and ice cream <u>with my friends</u>.

_____ I ate cake and ice cream <u>at the party</u>.

_____ I ate cake and ice cream <u>this afternoon</u>.

_____

_____

_____ The mother bought a <u>dress</u>.

_____ The mother bought a dress <u>for her baby</u>.

_____ The mother bought a dress <u>at the Little Bear Shop</u>.

_____ The mother bought a dress <u>yesterday</u>.

_____

_____

Sentence Building

Write a word or words on each line to make the sentences tell more and more. Draw a picture of the last sentence.

My _____ and I went to a _____.
     Who?   What?

My _____ and I went to a _____ at the _____.
     Who?   What?   Where?

My _____ and I went to a _____ at the _____
     Who?   What?   Where?
_____.
     When?

Sentence Building

Read the sentence parts. Write a word on each line
to make the sentence tell more. Draw a picture of the
last sentence.

1. We traveled _____.
   How?

2. We traveled _____ to see _____.
   How?   Who or what?

3. We traveled _____ to see _____ last _____.
   How?   Who or what?   When?

4. We traveled _____ to see _____ last _____.
   How?   Who or what?   When?

   at the _____.
   Where?

5. We traveled _____ to see _____ last _____
   How?   Who or what?   When?

   at the _____ because _____.
   Where?   Why?

Using Good Letter Form

Here is a letter written in good form.

Heading →

Greeting →

Body →

Closing →

Signature →

June 8, 2002

Dear Erin,
　Would you like to keep my pet snake for the summer? I can't take him to camp with me. His name is Sneaky. He likes to curl up in my pocket. Please let me know if you want him.
　　　　　　Your friend,
　　　　　　Becky

Look carefully at the five parts of the letter above. Then answer these questions.

1. What is in the heading? _____

2. Where do you see commas? _____

3. Besides the first words of sentences, what words begin with capital letters?

_____

4. What part gives the writer's name? _____

Using Good Letter Form

On the lines below, write these letter parts in good form. Put them in the right places. Use capital letters and commas.

june 13, 2002

dear becky

I'd love to take care of Sneaky. When can I get him?

your friend

erin

_____

_____

_____

_____

_____

_____

_____

Proofreading Practice
Friendly Letter

As you read the letter below, you will notice that there are errors in verb agreement, capitalization, and punctuation. Practice using proofreading marks to correct the errors. Use the proofreading marks on page 6 if you need help.

July 18 2002

dear mom and dad

I loves Funtime Camp! I is having a great time. I've learn how to paddle a canoe without tipping it over I can rides a horse, and I baits my own fishing hook. I catched four sunfish the other day, but we threw them back because they needed to grew.

At night we sings songs around the campfire and tells stories. Last night I eated six roasted marshmallows!

I'll telled you everything when you come to pick me up.

love

Doug

Writing a Thank-You Letter

It is good to say thank-you when someone does something nice for you or gives you a present. One way to say thank-you is to write a letter.

Maria liked the birthday present Uncle José gave her. She wrote this letter.

July 14, 2002

Dear Uncle José,
    The magic set you gave me is great. I practice with it every day after school. Now I can make a coin disappear. Soon I hope to make my brother disappear. Can you come over to see my magic show real soon?

Your niece,
Maria

Check the ways Maria lets her uncle know she likes his gift.

___ She says she likes it.

___ She tells how she uses it.

___ She says it isn't special.

___ She invites him to share the fun.

Write On Your Own

Think of someone you'd like to thank. Write that person a letter on a separate sheet of paper. Here are some things you might thank someone for: driving you somewhere, making you something good to eat, telling you stories, being your friend.

Addressing Envelopes

Now that you have learned how to write a letter, you need to learn how to address an envelope. In the upper right corner of the envelope, write your name. Below your name, write your street address. The next line should include your city, state, and Zip code. In the center of the envelope, write the name of the person to whom you are writing. On the line below the person's name, write that person's street address followed by the person's city, state, and Zip code. Remember to capitalize the names of people and places. Also notice the comma placed between the city and state.

Miss Angela Jones
3434 Maple Drive
Columbus, OH 12345

Mr. and Mrs. David Smith
2642 Newberry Street
Indianapolis, IN 67890

Look at the envelope below. Correct the capitalization and punctuation. Use the envelope above to help you.

dr. justin cook
1928 riverbend road
jonesboro ak 32145

ms. patricia nilson
709 fisher street
austin tx 78438

Getting Started with the Writing Process

Writing is like drawing a picture. Follow the steps of the writing process, and you will write a good description.

1. **Select** a topic you know. Look around you for ideas. Draw or write about whatever you see. Let's say you decide to write about your home. Write *home* on your paper and circle it. Draw smaller circles around the bigger one.

2. **Collect** your ideas by closing your eyes and thinking about your home. Write the words you think of in the smaller circles. Don't worry about spelling yet.

3. **Connect** or group the words in the small circles that go together or tell about the same thing.

4. **Draft** the words you connected by putting them into sentences. Try to describe your home so that someone who reads your description can see it clearly in his or her mind.

5. **Revise**, or change, anything that doesn't fit when you read the description aloud. Ask a parent or friend to help you find mistakes.

6. **Proofread** your final copy aloud. If you find any mistakes, correct them.

Tips for Your Own Writing:

- **Select** a topic that you like and **collect** your ideas.
- **Connect** your ideas that tell about the same thing.
- **Draft** your ideas into sentences.
- **Revise** by making changes and fixing mistakes.
- **Proofread** your paper aloud.

Getting Ideas

You can get writing ideas from looking, listening, reading, drawing, or imagining. When you are playing, it is easy to decide what to play. Why? You look around and play with whatever you have. You use your imagination.

Your writing ideas come the same way. Look around. Write about what you know or like. Make a list. Circle what you like the most.

For example, try writing the names of three people, things, or animals you know about. Circle the one you know or like the best. The circled word will be the main idea of your piece of writing. Draw five or more lines with smaller circles at the end of them. Next, write something that tells about or describes the word you circled. Does your paper look anything like this?

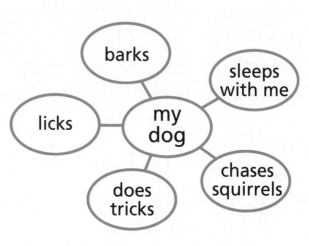

Now you have enough ideas to write a piece. Tell what your writing is about by stating the main idea in the beginning sentence. Then, just write about each idea in the smaller circles. As you write, add ideas as they come to mind.

Tips for Your Own Writing:

• Make a list of things that interest you.
• Circle the one that you know about the most.
• Draw circles for five words or phrases that tell about the main idea.
• Write your piece, putting your main idea in the first sentence.

Writing a Paragraph

A paragraph has one main idea. All of the sentences in a paragraph tell about or give clear details about the main idea. They are also organized in a proper order. Read the following paragraph about an airplane ride.

> *Courtney and I took our first plane ride. We sat in our seats and fastened our seat belts. We thought our airplane ride was exciting.*

The sentences are all in the proper order; however, by adding more details you can make it more interesting. Imagine what you might hear and do on an airplane ride. Read the following paragraph to see how more details can make a paragraph more interesting.

> *Courtney and I nervously prepared for our very first plane ride. The engines were revving up as we sat down and fastened our seat belts. The plane began backing up, and soon we were zooming down the runway. Up in the air and over the clouds we flew. Our ears plugged up and it was hard to hear. All too soon, our ride was over. We thought our ride was about the most exciting thing we'd ever done.*

Which paragraph is more interesting? Which one gives you a clearer picture of what the writer was experiencing? The second one, of course! When you write, try to "show," not "tell," your story.

Tips for Your Own Writing:

- Make sure each sentence in your paragraph tells about or gives clear details about the main idea.
- Check to make sure that your paragraph "shows" the reader what you are trying to say.

Proofreading Checklist

Did you ever say to yourself, "I didn't write that!" as you read your paper aloud? Sometimes we don't write what we **think** we are writing. This is why we **proofread**, or check, as part of the writing process.

Here are some things to check for:

1. Read your paper aloud and look for missing or extra words.
2. See if all proper nouns and beginnings of sentences are capitalized.
3. Check for misspelled words.
4. See that each sentence ends with the proper punctuation.

Have you ever been asked to help find something for someone, and you find it right away? In proofreading, you ask someone to help you find errors you didn't see yourself.

After you have checked your paper for correct spelling, capital letters, and punctuation, it is time to prepare a neat, final draft and proofread it.

See how the proofreading marks were used to mark the mistakes in the following paragraph.

Last night a small noise woke me up. i quickly sat up in bed. My heart was pounding! What could that be? then I heard another sound. "Meow!" said a little voice. It was just my cat!

Tips for Your Own Writing:

- Read your paper aloud and look for one type of mistake at a time.
- Check to see if any words are missing and if each sentence makes sense.
- Check for capital letters.
- Check for correct spelling and punctuation.

Description in Stories

When we tell a story, we use a lot of **vivid** words to make the story seem more real. Words like *soft, bubbly, long, smooth, brown, short, sad,* and *quiet* are some of the words we can use to describe a person, place, or thing. When we use descriptive words, we end up with a much better story.

Below are two ways to describe a room. The words in **bold italics** are description words. Which set of sentences gives you a better picture?

1. Jonathan has his own room. He likes the way it looks. He picked out his posters.

2. Jonathan has his own room. He likes its **light green** walls and **white** door. It is **small** but **cozy**. On his windows he has **green plaid** curtains. There is a **dark green**, **furry** rug near his bed. He has a **large**, **brown** desk. There are **bright** posters of zoo animals on the walls. The posters are Jonathan's favorite part because he picked them out himself.

The use of "sensory" words can help the reader better experience your story.

Sensory words you can use in your stories are:

See: *sparkling, spotted, streaked, foggy, green, shining*

Hear: *dripping, sloshing, shrieking, murmuring, crunching*

Smell: *bread baking, vanilla, clean hair, cut grass, gym locker*

Taste: *sour, sugary, lemony, creamy, peppery, sweet*

Touch: *prickly, silky, bumpy, bristly, furry, icy, fuzzy, slick*

Tips for Your Own Writing:

- Use description to help your reader experience your story.
- Use "sensory" words to help you with the description in your story.

Expository Writing–Writing a Report

Here are the five main steps for writing a good report:

1. Once you have chosen an interesting topic, you can make a **K-W-L** chart.

K	W	L
What I **K**now	What I **W**ant to Know	What I Have **L**earned

List all the things you know about your topic under **K**. Then, under **W**, list all the questions you have about your topic.

2. Your next step is to gather information at the library. As you read, list the most important things you learn about your topic under the **L** on your chart. Then look at your list of questions again. If there are some you have not found answers to, read some more and add notes under **L**. Put your facts in order. This will help you organize your ideas.

3. Next, decide which items under **K** and **L** go together.

4. Now you are ready to write your report. Write all of the important information you remember. After you finish, read your report. Change anything that is in the wrong order or doesn't make sense.

5. Check your work for mistakes in spelling, capitalization, and punctuation. Now write your final copy.

Tips for Your Own Writing:

- Choose a topic you like.
- Make a **K-W-L** chart.
- Read as much as you can about your topic and take notes.
- Use your notes and what you knew before to write about your topic.
- Read your report aloud to yourself and make necessary changes.
- Check your report for mistakes in spelling, capitalization, and punctuation.
- Share your report with a parent or friend.

Persuasive Writing

When you try to talk your parents into letting you stay up later, you are trying to *persuade* them. You want them to **believe** that it is okay. You also want them to **take action** by letting you stay up later.

When planning a persuasive writing piece, you should first think of all the reasons you have to get the reader to believe or to do what you, the writer, want him or her to do. You can write these reasons in the form of a letter to the person you are trying to convince. Include an introduction that states what you believe or want. Form a conclusion based on your reasons.

Suppose you are trying to convince your mother that you want in-line skates. Write her a letter telling her why you think you need and deserve in-line skates. What can you say that will convince her that you should have them? Also, think of why your mother wouldn't want you to have them and write reasons to convince her otherwise. For instance, if she said that she can't afford them, tell her you will get a job like cleaning yards to earn the money so that you can buy them yourself. You can also give reasons why the in-line skates would be helpful to you and to your family. If you know of any facts or information that would help to convince her, include those in your letter. Every reason or example you give should support your desire to have in-line skates.

Now put all of your reasons together in a way that makes sense. Revise and edit as many times as necessary. Proofread your final copy.

Tips for Your Own Writing:

- Think about what you would like.
- Gather and organize your reasons.
- Write an introduction.
- State your reasons.
- Write a conclusion based on your reasons.

Writing a Friendly Letter

Isn't it fun to get a letter in the mail? It makes you feel good. If you want to get a letter, you need to write one. The type of letter you might send to a friend or relative is called a **friendly letter**. You should have a purpose in mind when you write the letter. Maybe you would like to tell your grandparents about an exciting softball game you played in or tell a faraway friend what you have been doing since he or she moved.

Another type of letter you might write is a **thank-you letter**. It should tell what the thank-you letter is for. The following is an example of a thank-you letter:

January 20, 2002

Dear Aunt Patty,
    Thank you for sending me five dollars for my birthday. I used it to go to a movie and buy popcorn. I really liked the movie.
Love,
Kaleigh

No matter what your reason for writing a letter, it should be clearly written and include all of the necessary parts: the heading, a greeting, the body, a closing, and a signature. (See page 114.) If you are writing a return letter, answer each question that was asked of you.

Tips for Your Own Writing:

- Does your letter have all the necessary parts?
- Does the body of the letter give all the necessary information?
- Does your letter have the correct capitalization and punctuation?

An Invitation and an Envelope

An invitation can be written in letter form or on cards made especially to be used for invitations. If you are writing an invitation in a letter form, you have to be very careful to include all the necessary information. Those receiving invitations need to know the purpose first. For example, if you are inviting friends to a birthday party, they would need to know that because they would probably want to bring a gift.

Next, you need to let the people know when the activity is taking place. You not only need to tell them the date, but also the day and time. If you want a definite ending time, be sure to include that, also.

Then, add where the activity is taking place. For example, if it is being held outside, people need to dress according to the weather.

If the party is held for someone in particular, such as a birthday party, be sure to give the person's name. Otherwise, just give your name.

Lastly, decide if you want people to let you know whether or not they are coming. Be sure to include the initials R.S.V.P. and your telephone number if you decide you want to know.

When you mail your invitation, the envelope will look like this:

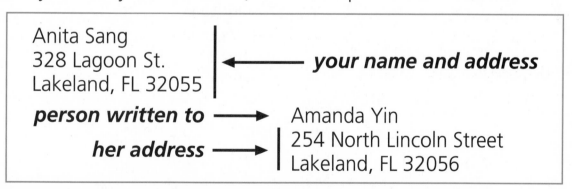

Tips for Your Own Writing:

- Make sure your invitation includes all of the necessary information.
- Don't forget to include your address on the envelope.

Postal State and Possession Abbreviations

Use these abbreviations on envelopes to be read by postal workers. In other writing, spell out the names of the states.

States

Alabama	AL
Alaska	AK
Arizona	AZ
Arkansas	AR
California	CA
Colorado	CO
Connecticut	CT
Delaware	DE
Florida	FL
Georgia	GA
Hawaii	HI
Idaho	ID
Illinois	IL
Indiana	IN
Iowa	IA
Kansas	KS
Kentucky	KY
Louisiana	LA
Maine	ME
Maryland	MD
Massachusetts	MA
Michigan	MI
Minnesota	MN
Mississippi	MS
Missouri	MO
Montana	MT
Nebraska	NE
Nevada	NV
New Hampshire	NH
New Jersey	NJ
New Mexico	NM
New York	NY
North Carolina	NC
North Dakota	ND
Ohio	OH
Oklahoma	OK
Oregon	OR
Pennsylvania	PA
Rhode Island	RI
South Carolina	SC
South Dakota	SD
Tennessee	TN
Texas	TX
Utah	UT
Vermont	VT
Virginia	VA
Washington	WA
West Virginia	WV
Wisconsin	WI
Wyoming	WY

District of Columbia	DC

U.S. Possessions

American Samoa	AS
Guam	GU
Puerto Rico	PR
Virgin Islands	VI

Capitalization
Sentences, People, and Pets

- The first word in a sentence is capitalized.
  Basketball is fun to play.
  Where is my basketball?

- The word **I** is capitalized.
  Do you think **I** can make a basket from here?

- The names of people and pets are capitalized.
  Monica **W**ilson is the coach of our basketball team.
  Carlos is the best player on our team.
  We met **P**atty and **L**isa at the game.
  My cat, **B**oots, likes to play with a ball of yarn.

Practice

Read the sentences below. From each pair of words in parentheses, choose the correct word and circle it.

1. (**Basketball,** basketball) is a fast and exciting sport.

2. In 1891 (james naismith, **James Naismith**) invented the game.

3. Ted and (i, **I**) practice our jump shots after school.

4. My dog, (**Tipper,** tipper), watches us shoot baskets in the backyard.

5. (the, **The**) Chicago Bulls is a championship team.

6. (michael Jordan, **Michael Jordan**) was my favorite player in the NBA.

7

Capitalization
People's Titles

- Names showing how you are related to someone are capitalized only if they are used in place of or as part of the relative's name.
  Fishing is **G**randpa's favorite hobby.
  Every summer, my **g**randpa takes us fishing.
  Last year, my **m**om caught a huge fish.
  This year, **M**om caught only a cold.

- Titles of respect used with names of persons are capitalized.
  Dr. Elizabeth Blackwell   **M**rs. Alvarez
  President Bush   **M**r. Peter Tepper
  Our class wrote letters to **M**ayor Busby.
  Our teacher, **M**s. Whitley, knows the mayor.

Practice

Read each pair of sentences. Underline the sentence that has the correct capitalization.

1. My Uncle has the same name as an American symbol.
   His name is Uncle Sam.

2. *The Cat in the Hat* was written by dr. Seuss.
   He was not really a doctor.

3. In *The Wizard of Oz*, Dorothy called out, "auntie Em."
   At the same time, her aunt worried about her.

4. A main character in *Peter Pan* was Captain Hook.
   He was the mean Captain of a pirate ship.

8

Capitalization
Places

- The major words in geographical names are capitalized.
  Chicago   Arizona   Italy
  Ohio River   Mount Rushmore   Pacific Ocean
  Lake Huron   Asia
  We flew directly from Lyon, France, to Manchester, England.
  The Rio Grande flows from the San Juan Mountains of Colorado
    to the Gulf of Mexico.
- The names of roads, places, and buildings are capitalized.
  Fairmont Avenue   Herald Square
  Washington Monument   White House
  The Sears Tower is taller than the Empire State Building.
  Columbia Hospital is on Central Avenue.

Practice

Rewrite the sentences. Look for two words in each sentence that should be capitalized.

1. We're planning to take a trip throughout north america.
   We're planning to take a trip throughout North America.

2. My mom works at broadview hospital.
   My mom works at Broadview Hospital.

3. My older brother wants to hike through the grand canyon.
   My older brother wants to hike through the Grand Canyon.

9

Capitalization
Dates and Holidays

- The names of the days of the week and the months of the year are capitalized.
  Monday   **W**ednesday   **S**aturday
  April   **J**uly   **O**ctober
  Mai goes to the library every **T**uesday afternoon.
  The hottest days of the summer are often in **J**uly.

- The names of holidays are capitalized.
  Labor **D**ay   **T**hanksgiving   **P**residents' **D**ay
  Flag **D**ay is celebrated on June 14.
  I look forward to **C**olumbus **D**ay every year.

- The names of the four seasons of the year are not capitalized
  spring   **s**ummer   **f**all   **w**inter

Practice

Read the sentences below. If the underlined part contains an error in capitalization, circle the word or words that should be capitalized.

We honor Americans who gave their lives for our country on Memorial (day.) Memorial Day is celebrated on the last (monday) in (may.) Some people call this holiday (decoration day.) Flowers and flag are placed on the graves of military personnel in spring. Many towns have parades on Memorial Day and (independence day) to honor people who served our country.

10

Proofreading Practice:
Capitalization

As you read the sentences below, you will notice that no words have been capitalized. Read each sentence carefully. Use the proofreader's mark (≡) to show which letters should be capitalized. Then rewrite each sentence with the correctly capitalized words.

1. sue attended a junior high school in kansas city, missouri, before coming here.

   Sue attended a junior high school in Kansas City, Misssouri, before coming here.

2. the president of the united states addressed a fourth of july celebration in detroit.

   The President of the United States addressed a Fourth of July celebration in Detroit.

3. last winter mom and dad took us skiing in the white mountains.

   Last winter Mom and Dad took us skiing in the White Mountains.

4. my teacher, miss adams, asked me to write the sentence on the board.

   My teacher, Miss Adams, asked me to write the sentence on the board.

5. the statue of liberty stands on liberty island in new york harbor.

   The Statue of Liberty stands on Liberty Island in New York Harbor.

6. my brother, my cousin, and i went on a vacation in kentucky.

   My brother, my cousin, and I went on a vacation in Kentucky.

11

Punctuation
Commas in Series, Dates, and Addresses

- A comma follows each item in a series except the last one.
  New York, Philadelphia, and Chicago have well-known city parks.

- A comma in a date separates the year from other words in a sentence.
  On July 4, 1976, the U.S. celebrated its 200th birthday.

- A comma in an address separates the name of a city and its state.
  The story takes place in Los Angeles, California.

Practice

Read the report below. Use the proofreader's mark (∧) to add commas after each word in a series.

There once was a Russian who made beautiful eggs for the czar, or ruler of Russia. Carl Fabergé made eggs that were covered with gold, silver, and other precious metals. Diamonds, pearls, and valuable jewels decorated other eggs. There was a surprise in each egg. A small golden carriage, a diamond-studded flower basket, or a royal crown may be found in a Fabergé egg. Today each egg is worth a great deal of money. Collectors own these special eggs, and they seldom offer the eggs for sale.

12

Proofreading Practice:
Commas

As you read about the colors of the flag of the United States, you will notice all the commas have been left out. Read the sentences carefully. Use the proofreader's mark (∧) to show where commas need to be added.

The Red, White, and Blue

Who made the first flag of the United States? No one really knows. A common belief is that Betsy Ross designed the first flag of the United States. She lived in Philadephia, Pennsylvania. A man named Francis Hopkinson claimed he designed the first one. Actually this argument has never been settled, but historians do not believe Betsy Ross was the designer.

Why is our flag red, white, and blue? There is no record of why the Continental Congress chose these colors. They seem appropriate since red is for courage, white is for purity, and blue is for justice and perseverance. The stripes stand for the original 13 colonies. The number of stars on the flag represents states admitted to the Union. As new states joined the Union, additional stars were added. At the present time there are 50 stars representing the 50 states. The 50th star represents Hawaii. On August 21, 1959, Hawaii was the last state to join the Union.

13

Possessives
Singular

- A **possessive noun** shows ownership or a relationship between two things. An apostrophe (') is always used to mark possessive nouns.
  Jane**'s** mountain bike is blue.
  The windowsill is the cat**'s** favorite place to sleep.

- A **singular possessive noun** shows ownership by one person or thing.
  Gary**'s** locker   the principal**'s** office

- To make a singular noun possessive, just add **'s**.
  the smile of the baby—the baby**'s** smile

Practice

On each line below, write the possessive form of the word in parentheses.

1. This is the house that Jack built. Is this __Jack's__ house? (Jack)
2. Mary has a garden. How does __Mary's__ garden grow? (Mary)
3. Little Boy Blue, come blow your horn. The __girl's__ flute broke. (girl)
4. Jack jumped over the candlestick. Did the __candle's__ flame hurt? (candle)
5. A wise old owl lived in an oak. Is the tree really the __owl's__ home? (owl)
6. Little Miss Muffet sat on a tuffet. Where was the __girl's__ chair? (girl)

14

Possessives
Singular and Plural

- A **singular possessive noun** shows ownership by one person or thing.
  the **ship's** captain   the **sailor's** uniform

- A **plural possessive noun** shows ownership by more than one person or thing.
  the **cities'** streets   the **states'** governors

- To make a plural noun that ends in **s** a possessive noun, add only the apostrophe.
  Girls—girls'   schools—schools'

- To make a plural noun that does not end in **s** a possessive noun, add an apostrophe and **s**.
  children—children's   teeth—teeth's

Practice

Change the underlined words to include a plural possessive noun. The first one is done for you.

        sea otters' faces
1. The cameras show the <u>faces of the sea otters</u>.
                             riverbanks' slopes
2. Otters sometimes play by sliding down the <u>slopes of the riverbanks</u>.
  pups' mother
3. The <u>mother of pups</u> watches them as they play.
                     sea urchins' shells for food
4. The mother otter cracks open the <u>shells of sea urchins for food</u>.
      babies' coats
5. She grooms the <u>coats of the babies</u> to keep them clean and waterproof.

15

Proofreading Practice:
Possessives

As you read the stories below, you will notice that apostrophes have not been added to show possessives. Read the sentences carefully. Use the proofreader's mark (⌄) to show where apostrophes need to be added. For extra practice, use the proofreader's mark (≡) to correct the capitalization.

The Pet Parade

  parkersville fun festival was held each year during the first two weeks in june. There were always a lot of fun activities. They included all sorts of contests, games, and carnival rides.

  the parkersville pet parade was held on the first saturday of the festival. All the neighborhood kids pets were ready for the parade. adams turtle had a picture of the united states flag painted on its back. kristens kitten, caramel, had a baby bonnet tied around its head and kept trying to get it off. ryans collie had been brushed until its coat sparkled, and it didn't mind the leash at all. justins bird was riding in its cage on the wagon justin had decorated. gabes llama was probably the most unusual pet of all. he hoped to win first prize.

16

Contractions
With *Not*

- A contraction is a shortened form of two words that are joined together. When the words are contracted, some letters are left out. An apostrophe takes the place of the letters that have been left out.
  My bicycle **does not** work. My bicycle **doesn't** work.

- Many contractions are made by putting together a verb and the word **not**.
  did not—did**n't**   are not—are**n't**
  do not—do**n't**   was not—was**n't**
  have not—have**n't**   could not—could**n't**
  has not—has**n't**   should not—should**n't**

- Two exceptions are:
  cannot—ca**n't**   will not—wo**n't**

Practice

Write a contraction above the underlined words in each sentence.

    aren't   **won't**   **can't**
We <u>are not</u> smiling. The car <u>will not</u> start, and the mechanic <u>cannot</u>
              couldn't
fix it until Friday. Antonia <u>could not</u> go to her piano lesson. Raphael
wasn't   **haven't**
<u>was not</u> able to go to baseball practice. I <u>have not</u> gone to the library
               shouldn't
to work on my report. We probably <u>should not</u> blame "Old Betsy."

17

Contractions
With *Verbs*

- Some contractions are formed by joining the words I, you, she, he, it, we, or they with a verb.

  I + am = I'm   we + are = we're
  I + have = I've   we + have = we've
  he + is = he's   you + are = you're
  she + is = she's   they + are = they're
  it + is = it's   they + will = they'll
  she + will = she'll

Practice

Write the letter of the words in Column B that matches the contraction in Column A.

	Column A	Column B
g	1. I'm	a. you are
e	2. they're	b. I have
a	3. you're	c. we are
b	4. I've	d. it is
c	5. we're	e. they are
d	6. it's	f. she will
f	7. she'll	g. I am

18

Homophones
Hear/Here, To/Too/Two

- Words that sound alike but are spelled differently and have different meanings are called **homophones**.

- *Hear* and *here* are homophones. **Hear** means "to listen to something." **Here** means "at" or "in this place." A good way to remember the difference is that **hear** has an "ear" in it.
  Can you **hear** it ring?
  I am going to put the telephone over **here**.

- Another example is to **to**, **too**, and **two**. To means "toward." **Too** means "also" or" more than enough." **Two** is the number between one and three.
  Maggie and Theresa went **to** the movies and ate **two** bags of popcorn. They drank lemonade, **too**.

Practice

Write the correct homophone in each sentence below.

1. "I'm going ___to___ the tennis court," Meg announced. (too, to, two)
2. Her younger sister, Peg, asked, "May I go, ___too___ ?" (too, to, two)
3. Meg said, "Sure, tennis is a game for ___two___ people." (too, to, two)
4. Meg added, ___Here___ , you may use my old racket." (Here, Hear)
5. Peg asked, "Do you ___hear___ Mom calling us?" (hear, here)

19

Articles
A, an, and the

- **A**, **an**, and **the** are useful words called <u>articles</u>. You can think of them as noun signals. They tell the reader there is a noun coming in the sentence.

- **A** and **an** tell about any person, place, thing, or idea.

- Use **a** with nouns that start with a consonant.
  a ball   **a** jump rope   **a** zebra

- Use **an** with nouns that start with a vowel sound.
  an egg   **an** oyster   **an** umbrella

- **The** tells about a specific person, place, thing, or idea.
  Give me **the** apple, please.

Practice

Underline each word (article) in the sentences below that signals any person, place, thing, or idea. Circle each word (article) that signals a specific person, place, thing, or idea.

We took my brother Jim to college last week. I had never been to <u>a</u> big university before. (The) campus was as big as <u>a</u> small town. Jim has classes in several different buildings. We visited <u>a</u> science building and (the) library. (The) dormitory where Jim lives is <u>a</u> ten-story building. (The) cafeteria and study rooms are on (the) first floor. (The) computer lab is on (the) fifth floor.

20

Recognizing Sentences

A sentence is a group of words that tells a whole idea.
A student has accidentally erased some of the words on the board.
Look at each group of words.

Is it still a sentence? Write **yes** or **no** in the ☐ .

Weekly Plans

yes	We will finish our science project by Friday.
no	This week's class helpers
yes	Please turn in your book report by Thursday.
no	Don't forget to
yes	Try to read for fifteen minutes at home each night.
yes	We will study fractions in math this week.
no	We will see a film about
no	Our weekly reading project will be
yes	Sign up for Sports Day.
no	Our guest speaker is
yes	Our math review is Wednesday.
yes	Leave your desk neat each day.

Choose **two** of the **no** lines. Add words to make complete sentences.

1. _____ Sentences will vary.
2. _____

21

Making Sentences

A sentence must tell a complete thought. Read the sentence parts. Draw a line to match each correct beginning and ending.

1. John and Patty attend — a band camp every summer.
2. The band camp lasts — for two fun-filled weeks.
3. All the kids bring — their own instruments.
4. John plays the tuba, — and Patty plays the flute.
5. Each day the kids — practice music together.
6. The teacher helps them — improve their performance.
7. On the last day, — they give a final concert.

22

Writing Sentences

A sentence must make sense. Read each sentence. Put an X on the two words which do not belong. Write the correct sentence on the line.

1. Last Saturday I ni~~ght~~ helped Granddad clean his ~~phone~~ attic.

   Last Saturday I helped Granddad clean his attic.

2. We found e~~xtra~~ three old trunks covered with ~~piece~~ cobwebs.

   We found three old trunks covered with cobwebs.

3. One trunk contained wi~~nter~~ Granddad's ~~skate~~ old photo albums.

   One trunk contained Granddad's old photo albums.

4. We un~~usual~~ found Granddad's old army uniform ~~size~~ in another trunk.

   We found Granddad's old army uniform in another trunk.

5. The last trunk was pl~~astic~~ filled with old clothes and books ac~~cident~~.

   The last trunk was filled with old clothes and books.

6. Granddad found a t~~welve~~ set of old trunk m~~ower~~ keys.

   Granddad found a set of old trunk keys.

23

Completing Sentences

A sentence needs a good ending. Read the beginning of each sentence. Write an ending to complete each sentence. Draw a picture of your complete sentence.

The kids are planning _____

The travelers stopped at _____

Sentences will vary.

The detective was surprised _____

The artist put a _____

24

Completing Sentences

A sentence needs a good beginning. Read the ending for each sentence. Write a beginning to complete each sentence. Draw a picture of each sentence.

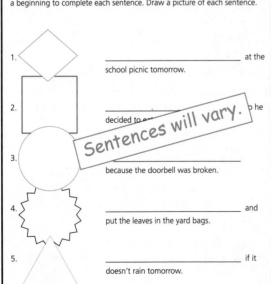

1. _____ at the school picnic tomorrow.

2. _____ he decided to e~~ ~~

   Sentences will vary.

3. _____ because the doorbell was broken.

4. _____ and put the leaves in the yard bags.

5. _____ if it doesn't rain tomorrow.

25

Writing Sentences

Look at each word. Write two words that tell something about the picture. Use the picture name and the two words in a sentence about the picture.

hot dog

_____   _____

skateboard

_____   _____

Sentences will vary.

van

_____   _____

football

_____   _____

26

Statements

- A statement is a sentence that tells something or gives information.
- A statement ends with a period.

Read the sign below. Then read the statements that tell about it.

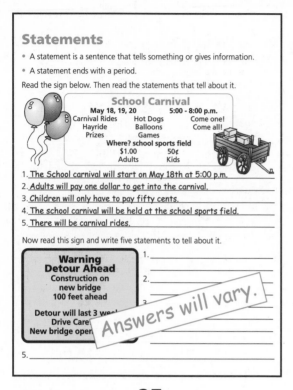

School Carnival
May 18, 19, 20   5:00 - 8:00 p.m.
Carnival Rides   Hot Dogs   Come one!
Hayride   Balloons   Come all!
Prizes   Games
Where? school sports field
$1.00   50¢
Adults   Kids

1. The School carnival will start on May 18th at 5:00 p.m.
2. Adults will pay one dollar to get into the carnival.
3. Children will only have to pay fifty cents.
4. The school carnival will be held at the school sports field.
5. There will be carnival rides.

Now read this sign and write five statements to tell about it.

**Warning
Detour Ahead**
Construction on
new bridge
100 feet ahead

Detour will last 3 weeks
Drive Care
New bridge open

1. _____
2. _____
3. _____

Answers will vary.

5. _____

27

Statements

A sentence can tell a lot about you. Begin at the START sign and write sentences that tell all about you. Write as many sentences as you can until you reach the center. (Use these questions to help you: How old are you? What color are your eyes? How tall are you? What are your hobbies?)

START

Sentences will vary.

28

Questions

- A question is a sentence that asks something.
- A question ends with a question mark.

Read each sentence. Put a question mark (**?**) in the circle at the end of each question.

DEPARTMENT STORE
BOOKS   TOYS   PETS   MUSIC   Pizza Hot Dogs

1. Would you like to go shopping ⃝?
2. Can we go to the mall ⃝?
3. How long can you stay ⃝?
4. I want to go to the department store ⃝
5. Where is the book store ⃝?
6. I am getting hungry ⃝
7. Would you like a pizza or a hot dog ⃝?
8. Do you want another piece of pizza ⃝?
9. My sister wants me to buy a record for her ⃝
10. Where is the escalator ⃝?
11. The pet store is on the second level ⃝
12. Are you going to buy new jeans ⃝?
13. I want to buy a toy for my little brother ⃝

Write three questions that you might ask at a mall.

1. _____
2. _____
3. _____

Questions will vary.

29

Questions

Reporters use many questions in their job. Look at each picture. If you were a reporter, what questions would you ask about each picture? Write two questions for each picture.

1. _____
2. _____

1. _____
2. _____

Answers will vary.

1. _____
2. _____

1. _____
2. _____

1. _____
2. _____

VOTE HERE

30

Spectrum Writing Grade 3

Exclamations

- An exclamation is a sentence that shows strong feeling or excitement.

- An exclamation ends with an exclamation mark.

The third grade is visiting the museum! Read each sentence. Put an exclamation mark (**!**) at the end of each exclamation.

1. That dinosaur is enor**m**ous!
2. Don't t**o**uch the mummy!
3. The guide i**s** very helpful
4. This stamp is worth a million d**o**llars!
5. Let's loo**k** around some more
6. I see the first airpl**a**ne that ever flew!
7. He**r**e is the world's largest diamond!
8. We have one more hour to look until l**u**nch
9. Look at the ancient writing **o**n that wall!
10. There is Abraham Lin**c**oln's coat!
11. I want to **b**uy a guidebook
12. This museum is a great place for **k**ids!

Look What We See

Write the underlined letter from each exclamation to learn what the class sees on its trip to the museum.

<u>m</u> <u>o</u> <u>o</u> <u>n</u>   <u>r</u> <u>o</u> <u>c</u> <u>k</u>

31

Exclamations

Look at each picture. Write an exclamation in each speech bubble to tell what the person could be saying.

Answers will vary.

32

Commands

- A command is a sentence that tells someone to do something.

- A command ends with a period.

Bob's dad is teaching his brother to drive. Read each sentence. Circle the number of each sentence that is a command.

1. Get in the **c**ar.
2. Put the k**e**y in the ignition.
3. Where are your glasses?
4. Lock your **c**ar door.
5. I will open the garage door.
6. Please fasten yo**u**r safety belt.
7. Re**l**ease the parking brake.
8. I see our neighbor, Mr. Owen.
9. Start the c**a**r.
10. Watch out **f**or the pets.
11. Look ca**r**efully around you.
12. Do you see any other cars?
13. **B**ack out of the driveway.
14. Will you drive carefully down the street?

Write the underlined letter from each circled sentence to see what command Bob gave his brother.

<u>B</u> <u>e</u>   <u>c</u> <u>a</u> <u>r</u> <u>e</u> <u>f</u> <u>u</u> <u>l</u>!
13 2   1 9 4 11 10 6 7

33

Commands

The kids at Camp Lagoona have not cleaned their cabin. Their leader is telling them what they have to do. Write eight commands that will tell the campers things they must do to clean the cabin.

1. _____
2. _____
3. _____
4. _____
5. _____
6. _____
7. _____
8. _____

Answers will vary.

34

Review: Types of Sentences

Read each sentence. Write the correct letter on each line:
S - statement **Q** - question **C** - command **E** - exclamation

<u>S</u> My town is fixing up the old theater.

<u>Q</u> Would the kids at school like to help?

<u>E</u> That's a terrific idea!

<u>C</u> Tell everyone to be here Saturday morning.

<u>Q</u> What should we bring?

<u>C</u> Bring a ladder and several paintbrushes.

<u>E</u> My dad has lots of extra blue paint!

<u>S</u> I will ask my teacher to help, too.

<u>S</u> We can begin to work when everyone arrives.

<u>C</u> Sweep and wax the stage floor.

<u>C</u> Put these costumes in the main dressing room.

<u>E</u> Look at this old ballet slipper!

<u>S</u> I will paint the entrance door black.

<u>Q</u> Can you repair the torn curtain?

<u>Q</u> Will you help the other kids clean the seats?

<u>C</u> Let's turn on the stage lights.

<u>E</u> The old theater is beginning to look great!

<u>Q</u> Will you be here on opening night?

<u>S</u> Our class is planning to sit together.

35

Review: Types of Sentences

Look at each picture. Write four sentences for each.
S - statement **Q** - question **C** - command **E** - exclamation

S _____
Q _____
C _____
E _____

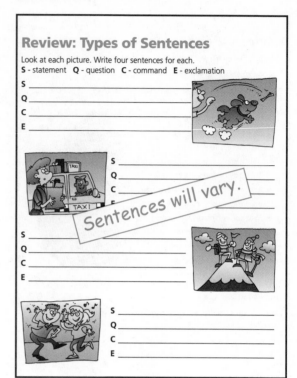

S _____
Q _____
C _____
E _____

Sentences will vary.

S _____
Q _____
C _____
E _____

S _____
Q _____
C _____
E _____

36

Writing with Your Senses

Look at the pictures below.
The five **senses** are **seeing**, **hearing**, **smell**, **taste**, and **touch**. Write answers to the following questions about the pictures.

1. What sense are the children in picture A using mainly?
   <u>smell</u>

2. What senses are the children in picture B using mainly?
   <u>seeing, taste</u>

37

Writing with Your Senses

- You know that details are small parts of a larger whole. You know also that a description is a group of sentences that tells details about something. When you gather details, you use your senses. Sometimes you use just one sense or mainly one sense. Other times, you may use all of your senses.

- Below is a description that uses four of the senses. Read the description. Then write the name of the thing being described.
  It is round and red. It feels smooth. It tastes sweet. It sounds crunchy when you bite it. It is an <u>apple</u> .

Write On Your Own

Think about a place you like to be. Or you may choose one of the places listed below. Then do the following things: First, write the senses **see**, **hear**, **smell**, **taste**, and **touch** across the top of another sheet of paper. Next, write details that tell about the place you chose under each sense. Finally, write your details together in a complete description. Be sure to write your description in complete sentences.

Ideas

1. your kitchen at holiday time

2. a park in the spring

3. your favorite store

38

Writing About Feelings

It is starting to rain. Do all the people in the picture feel the same way about the rain? On the lines below, tell how you think they feel and why.

1. The children feel _____

_____

_____

2. The woman feel_____ *Sentences will vary.*

_____

_____

_____

People can look at the same thing, like rain, differently. The way someone looks at, or views, something is called a point of view. Your point of view may come from where you stand. It may also come from the way you feel.

39

Writing About Feelings

Sentences can tell about feelings. Read the words in the box. Write three of the words to describe each person. Use the words to write two sentences about the person.

reserved	startled	grumpy
excited	unhappy	shy
shocked	bashful	happy
angry	thrilled	shaken

I feel . . . . 1. _____
excited
thrilled 2. _____
happy

I feel . . . . 1. _____
reserved
bashful 2. _____
shy *Sentences will vary.*

I feel . . . . 1. _____
shocked
startled 2. _____
shaken

I feel . . . . 1. _____
angry
unhappy 2. _____
grumpy

40

Nouns

- A **noun** is a word that tells who or what did the action or was acted upon in the sentence.
  The **ringmaster** wore a tall, shiny, black **hat**.

- A **common noun** names any person or place.
  woman   mountain   school

- A **singular noun** names one person, place, or thing and a **plural noun** names more than one.
  singular—town   plural—towns

- A **proper noun** names a particular person or place. Proper nouns start with capital letters.
  Eleanor Roosevelt   Southside School

- A **possessive noun** names who or what owns something.
  Pedro's basketball   the dog's bone   the actor's role

Practice

Circle the common nouns in the following paragraph. Underline the proper nouns.

(Dodoes) once lived on the (island) of Mauritius in the Indian Ocean. (Dodoes) were very unusual (birds.) Their (wings) were very tiny, so (dodoes) could not fly. A (dodo) was as big as a large (turkey.) These (birds) no longer exist.

41

Nouns
Writing Nouns that are More Exact

The person fed the animal.

The sentence above tells about both pictures. But it doesn't tell enough. The nouns person and animal aren't very exact. The next sentence uses more exact nouns to tell about picture 1.

The queen fed the lion.

What more exact nouns would tell about picture 2? Write a sentence with more exact nouns for picture 2 on the line below.

The clown fed the elephant.

_____

Read the list of nouns below. Then write two nouns that are more exact next to the nouns given. The first one is done for you.

1. building   _museum_

2. food   *Answers will vary.*

3. toy   _____   _____

42

Nouns
Writing Nouns that are More Exact

Read the sentences. Look at the nouns. Use more exact nouns to rewrite the sentences to make them more interesting. The first one is done for you.

1. The bird was in the tree.
   The robin was in the oak tree.

2. The animals walked across the land.
   _____

3. The liquid spilled on the floor.
   _____

4. The cookies were in the container.
   _____

5. The flower grew on the bush
   _____

6. The child p
   _____

7. Someone planted the vegetable.
   _____

8. The person picked out some clothes.
   _____

9. The car went down the street.
   _____

Sentences will vary.

43

Pronouns

- A **pronoun** is a word that takes the place of a noun or nouns. Pronouns help you avoid using the same nouns over and over. Pronouns change their spelling according to their use.
  John said that **John** was going to ride **John's** bike.
  John said that **he** was going to ride **his** bike.

- **I, you, she,** and **they** are examples of subject pronouns.
  Squanto was a member of the Pawtuxet tribe.
  He was a member of the Pawtuxet tribe.

- **Me, him, us,** and **them** are examples of object pronouns.
  Squanto showed the **colonists** how to fish.
  Squanto showed **them** how to fish.

- **My, your,** and **their** are examples of possessive pronouns.
  Squanto's friendship was important.
  His friendship was important.

Practice

Circle the pronouns in the sentences below.

Have you ever heard of Jane Addams? (She) wanted to help people living in poverty. There were no government agencies to help (them). Addams established a settlement house in Chicago. (It) was a place to receive help and learn new skills. The settlement house helped many people and made (their) lives easier.

44

Proofreading Practice: Pronouns

As you read the story below, you will notice that the pronouns have been used incorrectly. Read the sentences carefully. Circle the incorrect pronouns. Then write the correct pronouns above the words you have circled.

Shopping

Every year Mom and (me) go shopping together before school starts. It's lots of fun. We leave my brother at home. (Him) is not happy. Mom and (me) drive to the shopping mall and plan where to go first. (Her) wants to do the hard shopping first, so we do. I try on several winter coats, and we decide to buy the purple one with a fur-lined hood. Mom and (me) pick out gloves and snowpants to match the coat. Then mom and (me) go to try on jeans and sweaters.

Next, I lead the way into the school supplies store. I see some of my friends. (Them) are shopping with (them) moms, too. I pick up two red folders, a big bottle of glue, a box of forty-eight crayons, and twelve markers. (Me) can use last year's scissors, but I pick out a new bookbag with my favorite cartoon character on it. Mom remembers a ruler and writing paper as I get pencils and a big pink eraser. Mom and (me) go to the car loaded down with shopping bags.

45

Adjectives
Writing with Interesting Adjectives

The plane is taking off.

The sentence above tells something about the picture. But it doesn't tell much. It would tell more if it used comparing words. Comparing words tell how things are alike or different. A shorter name for comparing words is adjectives.

Now read the two sentences below that use adjectives to tell more about the picture above. Then underline the adjectives in each sentence.

1. The huge, bright, new plane is taking off.
2. The tiny, clumsy, old plane is taking off.

Underline each adjective in the next group of sentences.

1. Daisy got a shiny, blue bicycle for her birthday.
2. It had a large basket on the handlebars.
3. Last week she took her fluffy kitten for a ride.
4. First, Daisy wrapped the kitten in a soft, green blanket.

46

Adjectives
Writing About an Object

- Some words always describe things. Words like *smooth, soft*, and *loud* are describing words. You already know a word that means a describing word. That word is *adjective*.

  Look at the picture. Think about the cat. Then circle the adjectives below that describe the cat.

  square　(fluffy)　(soft)　mad
  black　wet　sad　(furry)

  Now think of two more adjectives that describe the cat. Write those adjectives below.

  1. ___ *Answers will vary.* ___

Write On Your Own

On another sheet of paper, write the name of your favorite food, toy, and clothing. Next to each favorite thing, write three adjectives that describe it. Remember to think about your five senses. After you have written your adjectives, choose one of the things to describe. Finally, write four or more sentences that describe your favorite thing. You may use the adjectives below.

Adjectives				
playful	speedy	noisy	cold	tasty
furry	quiet	brown	sharp	sweet
colorful	red	bright	soft	yummy

47

Adjectives
Writing Better Sentences

- Special words can make a better sentence.

  Read each sentence. Write a describing word on each line to make the sentence more interesting. Draw a picture of each sentence.

  1. The planet orbits the sun.

     The _____ planet orbits the _____ sun.

  2. We collected shells along the ___

     We collecte ___ *Answers will vary.* the

  3. The team scored points.

     The _____ team scored _____ points.

  4. Six roses were in the vase.

     Six _____ roses were in the _____ vase.

48

Review: Adjectives and Nouns

A sentence can tell about a specific thing. Write a size word, a color word, and a name of a thing on the lines to complete each sentence. Then draw the missing thing in the pictures. The first sentence has been done for you.

1. Lisa found a __small__ , __orange__ , __kitten__ by her front door.
   size　color　thing

2. Paul saw a _____ , _____ , _____ by the boat.
   size　color

3. The winner wore a ___ *Answers will vary.* ___ around his neck.

4. A _____ _____ was standing by Pete's sleeping bag.
   size　thing

49

Adverbs

- Adverbs can describe verbs. They tell when, where, or how an action happens.
  The concert will start **soon**. (Soon tells when.)
  The tuba player sits **here**. (Here tells where.)
  The drummer plays **loudly**. (Loudly tells how.)

- Adverbs can describe adjectives. They usually answer the question how or to what degree.
  quite handsome　**too** small　**rather** sweet
  My **really** naughty dog chews **very** old slippers.
  How naughty is my dog? **Really** naughty.
  How old are the slippers? **Very** old.

- Adverbs can also describe other adverbs.
  very quickly　extremely slowly　awfully quietly

Practice

Circle the adverb that describes the verb in bold type. Then circle the question that the adverb answers.

1. The game **started** (early) in the afternoon.　How?　(When?)　Where?
2. The Tigers (confidently) **took** the field.　(How?)　When?　Where?
3. The batter **walked** (slowly) to home plate.　(How?)　When?　Where?
4. The pitcher **threw** (there).　How?　When?　(Where?)
5. The batter (easily) **hit** the ball.　(How?)　When?　Where?
6. The crowd **applauded** (loudly).　(How?)　When?　Where?

50

Adverbs

Writing with More Exact Adverbs

Read the sentence below.

The snake is crawling **quietly outside now**.

Now write answers to the questions below.

1. Which one of the underlined words tells how the snake is crawling?

   quietly

2. Which word tells where the snake is crawling? outside

3. Which word tells when the snake is crawling? now

Adverbs are words like those underlined above. Adverbs tell **how**, **where**, and **when**. Find the adverbs in the sentences below. Underline each one.

1. I found my slipper <u>outside</u> <u>today</u>.
2. Rags was chewing it <u>happily</u>.
3. I yelled <u>loudly</u>, and he ran.
4. He ran <u>upstairs</u> and hid.
5. <u>Later</u>, I found him sleeping <u>peacefully</u>.

51

Verbs

- A **verb** is a word that shows action or expresses a state of being. Every sentence must have a verb. A verb such as **Go**! can be a one-word sentence. **Jump**, **shoot**, **listen**, and **read** are action verbs. **Am**, **are**, **is**, **was**, **were**, **be**, **being**, and **been** are all forms of the verb **be**. They tell what someone or something is, was, or will be.

- A **present tense verb** shows action that happens now.
  The farmer **plants** corn in early spring.

- A **past tense verb** shows action that happened earlier.
  The farmer **planted** beans in that field last year.

- A **future tense verb** shows action that will happen.
  Next year, the farmer **will plant** barley.

Practice

Underline the six verbs in the paragraph below. Write a more interesting verb above each verb to make the paragraph more interesting.

Suggested answers given.

> Woolly mammoths <u>walked</u> [roamed] on Earth more than three million years ago. These creatures <u>were</u> [grew] about eleven feet tall. They <u>seemed</u> [looked] like hairy elephants. Mammoths <u>had</u> [ate] moss, grass, and twigs. Early humans <u>killed</u> [hunted] the woolly mammoth for food and clothing. The last woolly mammoths <u>ended</u> [died] about ten thousand years ago.

52

Verb Agreement

- The verb has to agree with the subject of the sentence. This means that they must both be either singular or plural.

- Usually if the subject is singular, or the pronoun **he**, **she**, or **it**, add **-s** or **-es** to the verb.
  Dad **remembers** when few homes had TV sets.
  He often **reads** to my little brother.

- If the subject is more than one, or the pronoun **I**, **you**, **we**, or **they**, do <u>not</u> add **-s** or **-es** to the verb.
  My parents always **watch** the news on TV.
  I **ride** my bike to school.

Practice

Write the verb on the line that correctly completes each sentence.

1. Adam __works__ on the new computer. (works, work)
2. He __uses__ it to do his homework. (use, uses)
3. His brothers __play__ games on it. (plays, play)
4. His mom __writes__ stories on it. (writes, write)
5. His sister __types__ reports for school. (type, types)
6. Computers __make__ many jobs easier. (makes, make)

53

Regular Verb Tense

- **Tense** is a word that means "time." The tense of a verb tells you when the action takes place.

- A verb in the **present tense** shows action that happens now.
  The soccer players **kick** the ball toward the net.

- A verb in the **past tense** shows action that already happened. Add **-ed** to form the past tense of most verbs.
  The soccer players **kicked** the ball toward the net.

- To form the past tense of verbs that end in **e**, drop the **e** and add **-ed**.
  rake—rak**ed**   place—plac**ed**   taste—tast**ed**

Practice

Write the past tense of the verb in parentheses.

1. We __walked__ to the movies. (walk)
2. We didn't know that Len's dog __followed__ us. (follow)
3. We didn't notice that people __pointed__ at us. (point)
4. We finally __turned__ around. (turn)
5. Skipper __carried__ a dollar bill in his mouth. (carry)

54

Irregular Verb Tense

- Some verbs are special. They do not end in **-ed** to show past time. These verbs are called **irregular verbs** because they do not follow the pattern for forming the past tense. They have one special spelling to show past time.

  Erica **takes** us to the city each month. (present)
  Last month, she **took** us to the art museum. (past)
  We usually **ride** the train to the city. (present)
  On our last trip, we **rode** the bus. (past)

- Other irregular verbs include:

break—broke	begin—began	
come—came	do—did	draw—drew
eat—ate	make—made	think—thought
write—wrote	say—said	catch—caught
run—ran	grow—grew	win—won
give—gave	spring—sprung	buy—bought

Practice

Write the past tense of the verb over each underlined irregular verb in the sentences below.

> Julio <u>run</u> [ran] in a 5K race last week. He <u>think</u> [thought] that he would win. Tanya <u>come</u> [came] from behind and <u>catch</u> [caught] up with Julio. Tanya passed him and <u>win</u> [won] the race. She <u>break</u> [broke] the school record. Julio <u>do</u> [did] not feel bad about losing the race. He <u>say</u> [said] he will try harder next time.

55

Verbs

Writing with Interesting Verbs

The canoe **tipped**, and the boy **fell** into the water.

The words that are underlined in the sentence above are called verbs. Verbs tell action or help make a statement in other ways. If you choose exact verbs, they will help you say just what you want to say.

Read the sentences below. Then underline each verb.

1. Jan <u>danced</u> on the stage.
2. A frog <u>jumped</u> into my soup.
3. The squirrel <u>scurried</u> up the tree.

The most exact verbs make the most interesting sentences. Read the list of verbs below. Then write two verbs that are more exact next to the verbs given. The first one is done to show you how. *Suggested answers given.*

1. ran	sprinted	raced
2. walked	strolled	sauntered
3. ate	gobbled	consumed
4. talked	chatted	gossiped

56

Writing with Interesting Verbs

Look at the picture below. There is lots of action. On the lines below, tell what is happening in the picture. Use exact verbs to make your sentences interesting.

Sentences will vary.

57

Comparisons

- **Adjectives** are words that describe nouns.
- The ending **-er** is added to most adjectives that compare two people, places, or things. The ending **-est** is added to most adjectives to compare more than two people, places, or things.
  A coyote can run **faster** than a bear.
  The cheetah is the **fastest** animal of all.
- If the adjective ends with an **e**, drop the **e** before adding the **-er** or **-est** ending.
  large   larg**er**   larg**est**
- If the adjective ends with a single vowel and a consonant, double the consonant and add the **-er** or **-est** ending.
  big   bigg**er**   bigg**est**
- If the adjective ends with a consonant and **y**, change the **y** to **i** before adding **-er** or **-est**.
  tiny   tin**ier**   tin**iest**
- Some long adjectives use **more** and **most**.
  beautiful   **more** beautiful   **most** beautiful

Practice

Write the correct adjective on each line.

1. We just had the __hottest__ summer in history. (hotter, hottest)
2. Dad was __happier__ about the weather than we were. (happier, happiest)
3. His roses were __more beautiful__ than ever. (more beautiful, most beautiful)

58

Comparisons of Pictures

- When we compare things, we tell how they are alike or how they are different. The sentences beside the pictures are comparisons.

  Study the pictures. Then read the comparisons. Finally, underline the comparisons that best tell about the pictures.

1.
   One player is taller.

   One player is thinner.

2.
   One animal is longer.

   One animal is smarter.

3.
   The boy and girl are the same height.

   The boy is in the fifth grade.

Write On Your Own

On another sheet of paper, draw two sets of pictures. Draw the pictures in each set so that you can write comparisons for them. Then write a comparison for each set. Be sure to write your comparisons in complete sentences. You can use these words to get you started.

Words Used in Comparisons

more	fewer	louder	less
faster	same	bigger	higher

59

Comparisons Using er and more

Miff   Thor

Miff is <u>smaller</u> than Thor.   Thor is <u>larger</u> than Miff.

Both sentences above are comparisons. You already know that comparisons tell how things are alike or different. Some comparing words add **er** to their ends to make comparisons.

    small—small**er**   tall—tall**er**   high—high**er**

Now read the next sentence.
    A feather bed is **more comfortable** than a bed of nails.

What are the words that make the comparison in this sentence? Words like comfortable use the word **more** to make comparisons. Most long words use the word **more** to make certain comparisons.

    beautiful—more beautiful   important—more important
    dangerous—more dangerous

Using the list of comparing words, write two comparisons for the picture below. Add **er** to the correct words. Use **more** with longer words.

small	fancy	new
long	short	
comfortable		
beautiful		

Answers will vary.

60

Comparisons Using est and most

- Read the following paragraph.

  Flora is the clever**est** magician I know. She can do the **most** wonderful tricks. Her new**est** trick is to make herself disappear. Too bad she hasn't learned how to make herself appear again!

Cleverest, **newest**, and **most wonderful** are all forms of comparisons. They compare more than two things. When comparing more than two things, add **est** to the ends of short comparing words. But use the word **most** before longer comparing words.

Read the following comparing words. Write the word **two** beside those that can compare two things. Write the words **more than two** beside those that can compare more than two things.

1. greatest   *more than two*

2. greater   *two*

3. most wonderful   *more than two*

Write a comparison sentence for each comparing word below. Write each comparison so that it compares more than two things. The two forms are done to show you how.

thoughtful   *Harry is the most thoughtful person I know.*

great   *That was the greatest time of my life.*

1. old _____

2. delicious _____   *Sentences will vary. Make sure comparison forms are used correctly: oldest, most delicious, tallest.*

3. tall _____

61

Comparisons
Review

- Some comparing words drop, add, or change letters when they change form. For example: funny, funn**ier**, funn**iest** — large, larg**er**, larg**est**. If you are not sure of the spelling, check your dictionary.

Write three comparisons for the picture below. You may use the following comparing words or think up your own: large, big, small, little. Be sure to check your spelling.

1. _____

2. _____   Sentences will vary.

3. _____

Write On Your Own

Pretend you are the judge at a costume party. You have to choose the funniest costume, the ugliest costume, and the most unusual costume. On a separate sheet of paper, write five or more sentences that will tell about the costumes. Be sure to use the correct form for each comparison you write.

62

Comparisons Using like and as

• Look at the picture. Then read the sentences below that tell about it.

My horse runs **like the wind.**
My horse runs **as fast as the wind.**

• Another way to compare things is to use the words **like** or **as**. When used in comparisons, the words **like** and **as** tell how things compare. This type of comparison is also known as a **simile.**

Read the sentences about the picture again. Then answer the following questions.

1. To what are the sentences comparing the way the horse runs?
   the wind

2. How many things are being compared in the first sentence?
   two

3. How many things are being compared in the second sentence?
   two

Read the following comparisons. Then write your own comparisons by finishing the phrases below.

Daria's smile is like a slice of watermelon.
She is as thin as a wrinkle.

1. Chico laughs like _____ Sentences will vary. Make sure that
2. Our car is like _____ comparisons using like and as have been
3. The pudding looks like _____ written.

63

Writing Similes

A sentence can use fun expressions. Read each sentence. Write a word on each line to complete the sentence. Draw a picture of each sentence.

1. The _____ is as slow as a _____

2. My _____ is as quick as a _____ .

Answers will vary.

Read each sentence. Finish the sentences with interesting comparisons. The first two are done for you.

1. She worked _____ like a horse.
2. She had eyes _____ like twinkling stars.
3. The tree was as straight as _____
4. The snow was as cold as _____
5. The water is as warm as _____
6. The boy was as strong _____
7. He played basketball like _____
8. The sun was as hot as _____

Answers will vary.

64

Comparisons Using good and bad

Read the sentences below that tell about the picture.

Sam has a **good** seat.
Felicia has a **better** seat than Sam.
Yolanda has the **best** seat of the three.

Now read these sentences.
Marybeth's bike is in **bad** shape.
Nazir's bike is in **worse** shape than Marybeth's.
Frank's bike is in the **worst** shape of the three.

Read the sentences above again. Then answer the following questions. Write your answers on the lines.

1. What word compares two seats? _____ better
2. What word compares more than two seats? _____ best
3. What word compares two bikes? _____ worse
4. What word compares more than two bikes? _____ worst

65

Comparisons Using good and bad

Using the two forms of good and bad that you have learned, write your own comparisons on the lines below. The examples below will show you how.

Good
good   John is a **good** singer.
better Manny is a **better** singer than John.
best   Estella is the **best** singer of the three.

Bad
bad   Angela has a **bad** cold.
worse   Glen has a **worse** cold than Angela.
worst   Melinda has the **worst** cold of the three.

1. good _____
2. better _____
3. best _____
4. bad _____
5. worse _____
6. worst _____

Sentences will vary.

Write On Your Own

On another sheet of paper, write about something you saw or something that happened to you. Using a comparison of **good** or **bad,** write at least five sentences. You may use the ideas below or you may think up your own.

The Best Summer Vacation   The Worst Storm

66

Polishing Your Writing

Two people went there. They saw some funny things. They enjoyed it very much.

The story above doesn't tell very much. But you can make it more interesting when you rewrite it. You can use exact nouns and verbs. You can add adjectives to describe people and things. You can add adverbs to tell where, when, or how. You can check to see that all verbs tell about the same time.

Now rewrite the story at the top of the page. Make it as interesting as you can.

Answers will vary.

67

Writing About a Person

- You know some words that describe objects. There are words that describe people, too.

Write the word or word group from the list under the picture of the person it describes. Some words may not fit either person.

Words That Can Describe People

tall	curly hair	wearing glasses
short	long hair	flowered dress
thin	dark hair	light hair
freckles	short hair	long pants

short	tall
long hair	thin
wearing glasses	curly hair
flowered dress	short hair

68

Writing About a Person

Write four or more sentences that describe the picture above. Try to describe everything that the picture shows. Tell how the boy looks, how he is dressed, and how he feels.

Answers will vary.

Write On Your Own

Think about one of your favorite people. Think about how that person looks and how he or she acts. Think about what that person does best. Think about why you like that person. Then, on another sheet of paper, write five sentences that describe your favorite person. Remember to use exact nouns, verbs, and adjectives.

69

The Writing Process

- The **Writing Process** is a set of steps to help you make your writing the best it can be. Read about the **Writing Process** below. You'll get to try each step on your own in the pages that follow.

1 Prewriting
Prewriting is what you do before you write. It is a way of collecting your thoughts and ideas for what you want to write about. Sometimes it is called **brainstorming**.

2 Drafting
Your first try at a piece of writing is called a **rough draft**. When you write a rough draft, don't worry about spelling and punctuation. Just get your writing started!

3 Revising
Revising means to make corrections. When you revise your writing, you want to be sure it makes sense. You want to make sure nothing is missing. This is also a good time to check that you have used interesting words.

4 Proofreading
When you **proofread** your writing, you are looking for mistakes. Now, it is time to check your spelling, punctuation, and to make sure you capitalized words correctly.

5 Publishing
When you **publish** your writing, you are ready for people to read it! You should use your best handwriting and a nice clean piece of paper. Or, you can type your piece of writing on a computer.

70

Prewriting

- The first step of the writing process is called **prewriting**. **Pre-** means "before," so **prewriting** means "before writing." This is the time when you get to **think** about writing. Here are some questions you can ask yourself when you are **prewriting**:

What do I want to write about?
What do I know a lot about?
Where can I find information?
What are some words or ideas I can use for my topic?

Now let's practice doing some prewriting!

A topic for writing is **animals**. Can you answer these prewriting questions about **animals**? Write down whatever you think of.

What animals do I want to write about? _____

_____

What animal do I know a lot about? _____

_____

What are som_____ bout that animal? _____

_____

Where can I find more information about that animal? _____

71

Prewriting

Brainstorming helps you organize your ideas. Read each question. Write your ideas on the lines. Use your ideas to write five sentences about some of your favorite sports.

What are some popular sports?

1. _____ 3. _____ 5. _____
2. _____ 4. _____

What equipment is used?

1. _____ 3. _____ 5. _____
2. _____ 4. _____

Where are the

1. _____ 5. _____
2. _____ 4. _____

Sports Fun

1. _____
2. _____
3. _____
4. _____
5. _____

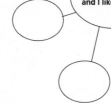

72

Prewriting

- Another prewriting method is **writing webs**, also called story webs or clustering. Again, you think of everything you can about a topic. Then you write each idea down like this:

cheese

spaghetti

corn

Answers will vary.

h

ice cream

Can you add two more ideas to this web?

73

Prewriting

Here is another topic for you. Can you fill in the web with words and ideas that you could write about?

Answers will vary.

Things my friends and I like to do

74

Prewriting

• Another kind of prewriting is called **freewriting**. It is just what it sounds like. You are free to write whatever comes to mind. You just start writing and keep going. Don't worry about what fits. Don't worry about spelling, capitalization, or punctuation. You can fix that later.

Freewriting lets your ideas come out! **Just write!**

Here is an example of freewriting.

I just wanted to help It was a hot day. Mom came in with lots of groceries. Shee needed help. I wanted to show her I was responsable. I got lots of stuff out of the bags. Some fell on the floor. I like cookies. Mom was happy.

Can you figure out what the topic was?
The young boy wanted to help his mother.

75

Drafting

• Step Two of the writing process is called **drafting**. It is time to take all of the ideas and words you came up with during prewriting and begin to write the real thing.

Choose one of your topics from any of the Prewriting pages. Write your ideas on the lines below. You may even have new ideas that you can add here. Remember, your prewriting only needs to be words or short phrases. You'll write complete sentences later when you practice drafting.

Answers will vary.

Using the ideas above, draw a picture of your topic.

Drawings will vary.

76

Drafting

Now it is time to practice **drafting**. Look at all of the ideas you have about your topic from page 76. Which ones go together?

Take the ideas and words and make complete sentences.

Example: (ideas)   cows, chickens, horses, goats

On the farm I see lots of animals. There are cows, chickens, horses, and goats.

Now write some sentences using your ideas from page 76.

Answers will vary.

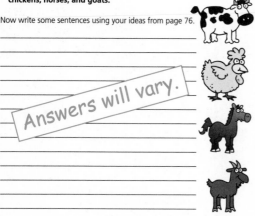

77

Rough Draft

All of the sentences you drafted on page 77 can be put in order to make a story. Can you put your sentences together so your story makes sense? Try it on the lines below:

Answers will vary.

78

Revising

- After drafting, it is time for step three of the writing process, **revising**. To **revise** means "to change."

Look closely at what you have written. You want to ask yourself questions like:

Does this make sense?
Have I used describing words (nouns, verbs, adjectives)?
Am I missing anything?
Does everything fit here?
Should I take something out?
Do I have things in a good order?

Then you **revise** the sentences until you have a better story. Don't worry about spelling, capitalization, or punctuation yet. That will come next.

Look at the sentences below. Revise each one to make it a more interesting sentence. Then draw a line to the number to show which sentence should come first, second, and third. *Sample sentences given.*

1 After school, Jon did something.
After school, Jon played soccer with his friends.

2 At bedtime, he read something.
At bedtime, he read a biography about his favorite baseball player.

3 In the morning, Jon ate something.
In the morning, Jon ate a bowl of cereal and a banana.

Just So You Know
Sometimes you will revise more than once before a sentence or story is really terrific.

79

Revising

Remember: When you **revise**, ask yourself these questions:

Does this make sense?
Have I used describing words (nouns, verbs, adjectives)?
Am I missing anything?
Does everything fit here?
Should I take something out?
Do I have things in a good order?

Look at the story you wrote on page 78. **Revise** it on the lines below.

Answers will vary.

How does your story look now? Do you like it better? Show your story to a parent or friend. Does he or she have any ideas to help you revise your story even more?

80

Proofreading

How do you like your story now? If you need to revise it more, use another sheet of paper.

When you are done **revising**, it is time for Step Four of the writing process, **proofreading**.

Now you can fix mistakes in

spelling
capitalization
punctuation

Here are some **proofreading marks** that will help you. See how they are used in the story below.

I went to schoool yesterday. I forgot my books. They were at home. Why did I forget them? My dog, scotty, was sleeping on them. miss jones didn't scold me. She was really nice to mee. Maybe Miss Jones has a dog at her house too.

Proofreading Marks
misspelling: ⬭
capitalize: ≡ ohio
add . . .
a period: ⊙
an apostrophe: ⅴ

81

Proofreading

It's time to practice proofreading. Remember: You are looking for mistakes in:

spelling	I ate for eggs. (four)
punctuation	Wait! You can't go there⊙
capitalization	scott caught a Fish in the lake.

The **proofreading marks** are here to help you.

Proofreading Marks
misspelling: ⬭
capitalize: ≡ ohio
lowercase: / Sister
add . . .
a period: ⊙
an apostrophe: ⅴ
a question mark: ?
an exclamation point: !

It's lunch time! We have fun eeting our lunch with louis. he does magick tricks for us. Look at how he makes my spoon disappear! Can he make it come back? I hope so. I want to eat my pudding. (eating, magic)

Proofread these sentences, too.

The clintonville cubs have a game on tusday. (Tuesday)
Who are they playing? I want too go watch tham. (to, them)
I'll go, too. Pick me up at twevle o'clock⊙ (too, twelve)

82

Proofreading

The more you practice proofreading the better your writing will be. Practice proofreading the sentences below. Write the corrected sentences on the lines.

when
I saw a huge moose (wen) we went camping⊙
I saw a huge moose when we went camping.

make
Did you (mak) a wish at the the wishing Well?
Did you make a wish at the wishing well?

friends
the playground is a Fun place for (freinds)
The playground is a fun place for friends.

bottle *right*
The Baby needs a (botle) of milk (rite) away!
The baby needs a bottle of milk right away!

story
It's time for bed. Will you read me a (storie)?
It's time for bed. Will you read me a story?

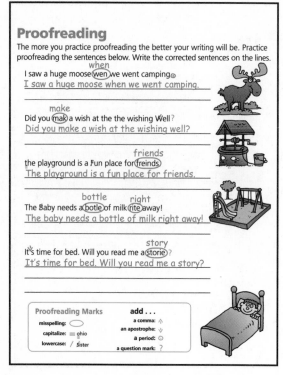

Proofreading Marks	add . . .	
misspelling: ⬭	a comma: ⋀	
capitalize: ≡ ohio	an apostrophe: ⋁	
lowercase: / Sister	a period: ⊙	
	a question mark: ?	

83

Publishing

• Step Five of the writing process is called **publishing**.
There are lots of ways to **publish** your writing. Look at the examples below.

How would you publish your writing?

Answers will vary.

84

Proofreading and Publishing

Now go back to your story on page 80. Look at what you wrote. Proofread your story for mistakes.

Now write the final draft on the lines below.

Answers will vary.

Now your writing is all done. You have fixed all of the mistakes. You have written or typed your writing neatly. It is ready for others to read. Show your story to a parent or friend. When you have done all these things, you have **published** your writing!

85

Writing the Main Idea of a Picture

Look at the picture. What is the picture about?

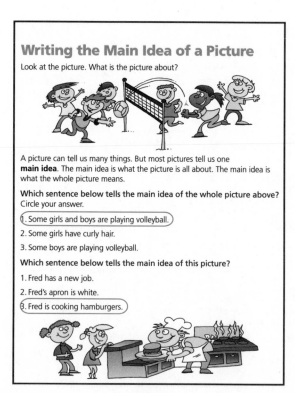

A picture can tell us many things. But most pictures tell us one **main idea**. The main idea is what the picture is all about. The main idea is what the whole picture means.

Which sentence below tells the main idea of the whole picture above? Circle your answer.

1. Some girls and boys are playing volleyball.
2. Some girls have curly hair.
3. Some boys are playing volleyball.

Which sentence below tells the main idea of this picture?

1. Fred has a new job.
2. Fred's apron is white.
3. Fred is cooking hamburgers.

86

Writing the Main Idea of a Picture

Draw a picture in the space below. Then write the main idea of your picture on the line.

Drawings will vary.

The main idea of my picture is: _____

Answers will vary.

Write On Your Own

On another sheet of paper, draw three more pictures. Then under each picture, write its main idea. You might want to use the ideas below. Or think up your own ideas for the pictures.

Ideas
Something that happens at school
Something that happens at home
Something that happens at play

87

Writing a Title

Look at the picture below.

A **title** is a name for a picture or story. It tells what the picture or story is all about. A title is a short way to tell the main idea of a picture or story.

Look at the picture again. Then read the titles below. Circle the title that best tells about the picture.

1. Sunny Day at the Park
2. Playing in the Park ⟵(circled)
3. Some People Don't Ride Bicycles

88

Writing a Title

Read this story.

First, Charlotte hit her toe when she jumped out of bed. Then she had no clean socks to wear. At breakfast she burned her toast. Then she spilled her juice on her homework. It was not a good beginning to Charlotte's day.

What title below best tells about the whole story? Circle your answer.

1. Charlotte's Day
2. The Burned Toast
3. A Bad Beginning for Charlotte ⟵(circled)

Read the next story. Think about its main idea. Then write a title for the story on the line below.

Have you ever seen a UFO? Some people think UFOs fly around. But nobody knows what they are. Nobody knows if they are real. Some people say they have seen UFOs. Other people say UFOs are a trick.

A good title for this story is: _____ Answers will vary.

Write On Your Own

On a separate sheet of paper, write your own story. Make it four or more sentences long. Then write a title for your story on the top line of your paper. You can use one of the ideas below. Or you can think up your own idea.

Man Wins Pancake Flipping Contest
Girl Invents New Glue
Elephant Escapes from Zoo

89

Writing Story Parts in Order

- Some stories are true. For example, most news stories are true. Most stories about real people's lives are true. Can you think of a story about a real person that is true?

- Some stories are not true. They are about what a writer has imagined. They are make-believe. For example, *Cinderella* is a make-believe story. Can you think of another make-believe story?

- Whether stories are true or make-believe, they all have a **beginning**, a **middle**, and an **end**. The beginning, middle, and end of a story are written in sequence. The beginning comes first, the middle comes second, and the ending comes last.

Read each story below. Then write **beginning**, **middle**, or **end** beside the correct part.

1. _beginning_ Vera picked up a large egg.
   end A baby bird hopped out of the egg.
   middle She broke it.

2. _middle_ Next, a snake came out of the man's basket.
   beginning First, the man began to play his horn.
   end Finally, the snake began to sway to the music.

90

Writing Story Parts in Order

Each group of sentences below can tell a story. But one part of each story is not finished. Write the beginning, middle, or end of each story. Then write the word **beginning**, **middle** or **end** beside the part you have written.

1. It began to snow in the early evening.
   It snowed all night.

   In the morning _____

   _____

2. Jamie and I built a large boat.

   We _____

   _____

   Then we la___ ___mall island with strange animals.

3. The mailman _____

   _____

   I opened the package as quickly as I could.
   I found a sweater with my name on it.

Sentences will vary.

Write On Your Own

On another sheet of paper, write a story that tells about the funniest thing that ever happened to you. Be sure your story has a beginning, a middle, and an end. Your story can be make-believe or true.

91

Story Sequence

A story needs a good ending. Look at the beginning and middle of this boy's dream. Write three sentences to tell what happened at the end. Draw a picture. Then write three sentences to tell what is happening at the beginning and in the middle.

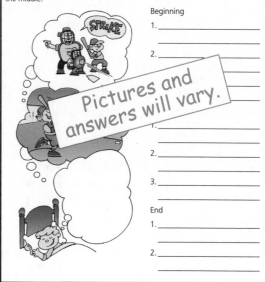

Beginning
1. _____

2. _____

Pictures and answers will vary.

1. _____

2. _____

3. _____

End
1. _____

2. _____

92

Writing the Main Idea of a Paragraph

Read the paragraph below.

   Fish sleep in different ways. Some sleep in the sand. Some sleep on their sides. Others sleep on their tails. One fish sleeps while standing on its head!

You know that pictures have main ideas. Well, paragraphs have main ideas, too. The main idea of a paragraph is what the paragraph is all about.

Read the paragraph about fish again. Then circle the sentence below that tells its main idea.

1. Fish are lazy.
2. (Fish sleep differently.)
3. Some fish sleep in the sand.

Read the next paragraph.

   I got up early. I jumped out of bed. Quickly, I washed and dressed. Then I ran down the stairs. I gulped down my breakfast. I couldn't wait to go on my first camping trip.

What is the main idea of the paragraph? Circle the best answer.

1. (I rushed to go camping.)
2. I ate a big breakfast.
3. I ran down the stairs.

93

Writing the Main Idea of a Paragraph

Write your own paragraph on the lines below. Make your paragraph at least four sentences long. You can choose one of the ideas below. Or you can think up your own idea.

   I love to go skiing.
   One day, I got lost while shopping.

_____

Answers will vary.

No write a se___ ___ on the lien below that tells the main i dea of your paragraph.

Write On Your Own

On another sheet of paper, write two paragraphs. Write one paragraph about something that truly happened. Write the other paragraph about something you can imagine might happen. Write "I imagine" above the make-believe paragraph. Write "This really happened" above the paragraph that is true. Then write the main idea of each paragraph below it. Here are some ideas you may want to use. Or you can think up your own ideas.

The last day of school   Building a tree house
The day I went sky diving   Finding a million dollars

94

Writing Paragraphs that Make Sense

What doesn't make sense in this picture?

Did you ever read something that didn't make sense? Something that doesn't make sense can juggle your mind. It can mix you up. A picture should make sense. A paragraph should make sense, too. A paragraph makes sense if all its sentences tell about the main idea.

Read the next paragraph. Think about the main idea as you read.

Tulips are my favorite flowers. I love to see the red, yellow, pink, and orange flowers in rows. Tulips tell me that spring is here. We have to stand in rows at school.

Answer the following questions about the paragraph. Write your answers on the lines.

1. What is the main idea of the paragraph? _____
   Tulips are my favorite flowers.

2. Which sentence doesn't make sense in the paragraph? _____
   We have to stand in rows at school.

3. Why doesn't one sentence make sense in the paragraph? _____
   It doesn't tell about the main idea.

95

Writing Paragraphs that Make Sense

Read the next two paragraphs. Then write your answers on the lines below each one.

Our neighbor told us about her trip to Europe. She traveled by boat. One night, she met a prince. She married him. I took a trip to Disney World. Then she decided she missed home too much. She flew on the fastest plane. She arrived home yesterday.

1. The main idea is: _____
   Our neighbor took a trip to Europe.

2. The sentence that doesn't make sense in the paragraph is: _____
   I took a trip to Disney World.

Tugboats are small boats used to move large ships. I'd like to sail a ship someday. A tugboat's engine is very powerful. The small boat can pull or push. It's fun to see tugboats moving big ships around.

3. The main idea is: Tugboats move large ships.

4. The sentence that doesn't make sense in the paragraph is: _____
   I'd like to sail a ship someday.

Write On Your Own

Use this main idea: "One day I put my shoes on the wrong feet." Or use your own main idea. Then, on a separate sheet of paper, write a paragraph using the main idea you have chosen. Remember: Use only sentences that belong with the main idea.

96

Writing Paragraphs that Make Sense

• You know that a paragraph is a group of sentences about one subject. Read the sentences in the paragraph. Put a line under the sentences that do not belong. Then write the correct sentences to make a paragraph.

Yesterday I tried out for the All-School Swim Team. I got up early to exercise and eat a good breakfast. The sweater was too big. Everyone met at the pool at 10:00 A.M. I finished my homework. The coach had us swim laps to warm up.
My sister's birthday is tomorrow. He divided us into small groups. Each group swam four strokes for him. I lost my new skateboard. The coach watched carefully and then made notes. Tomorrow he will announce the new team.

Yesterday I tried out for the All-School Swim Team. I got up early to exercise and eat a good breakfast. Everyone met at the pool at 10:00 A.M. The coach had us swim laps to warm up.
He divided us into small groups. Each group swam four strokes for him. The coach watched carefully and then made notes. Tomorrow he will announce the new team.

97

Writing Paragraphs that Make Sense

The main idea of a paragraph is also known as the topic sentence. You have practiced writing the main idea of a paragraph and learned that sentences in a paragraph make sense. Here is some more practice for you. Read each topic sentence. Write a paragraph about the subject in each topic sentence.

This morning my mom took me to shop for new clothes for school.

_____

Answers will vary.

Yesterday I got first pair of glasses.

98

Writing Paragraphs that Make Sense

Look at the picture. Write a topic sentence. Write other sentences to make a paragraph to tell about the picture.

Paragraphs will vary.

99

Proofreading Practice:

Writing Paragraphs that Make Sense

As you read the article below, you will notice sentences that do not belong. Read the sentences carefully. Circle the sentences that do not belong in the story.

The Changing Seasons

It takes the earth one year to go around the sun one time. Don't you wish the earth would move faster? The earth doesn't point straight up and down. The earth tilts a little to one side. The earth tilts on a pretend stick that goes through the earth from pole to pole. We call this "stick" the axis. It's because of the earth's tilt on its axis that we have different seasons. The tilt does not change as the earth circles the sun.

When the part of the earth you live on tilts toward the sun, you get more daylight hours and more direct heat from the sun. This would be the summer season. I think summer is the best season because you can go swimming. When your part of the earth begins to tilt away from the sun, you start to get less sunlight and less heat. We call this season fall. Fall is when football is played. You also have to rake the fallen leaves.

When the tilt of the earth is farthest away from the sun, you get the fewest daylight hours and heat from the sun. This is winter. Winter is fun when it snows.

When the earth's tilt once again begins to get closer to the sun, we get more heat and daylight hours. This is the season we call spring.

100

Writing Picture Stories

Look at the groups of pictures below. They can tell a story. Put each group of pictures in correct order so that they do tell a story. Write **first**, **next** or **last** under each picture to show the correct order.

first   last   next

next   first   last

When you put each group of pictures above in order, you put them in **sequence**. Sequence tells you what comes first, next, or last.

101

Writing Picture Stories

The pictures below are in sequence. They tell part of a story. Finish the story by drawing the last picture in the space.

Drawings will vary.

First   Next   Last

On each line below, write a sentence that tells about each picture above. Be sure that your sentences are in sequence.

First:

Next: Sentences will vary.

Last:

Write On Your Own

On another sheet of paper, draw your own picture story. Use at least three pictures for your story. Then write a sentence under each picture that tells about the picture. Be sure your pictures and sentences are in sequence. You can use the ideas below. Or you can think up your own idea.

Planning a Friend's Birthday Party
Practicing a Music Lesson
Feeding Your Baby Sister

102

Writing Sequence Words

"First, I go into the phone booth."
TELEPHONE

"Then, I use my super powers."
TELEPHONE

"Finally, I become super... frog?!"
TELEPHONE

Study the pictures above. The words that are underlined are **sequence** words. Sequence words tell when something happens. *First, then, next,* and *finally* are sequence words. Some other sequence words are *last, second, third, tomorrow, yesterday, before,* and *after*.

Read the lists of sequence words below. Then number each word to show which word tells first, second, or last. Use the numbers 1, 2, or 3.

2 middle   3 night
1 beginning   1 morning
3 end   2 noon

Find the sequence words in the next paragraph. Circle each one.

(First,) I gave the crazy monkey a banana. (Then) she peeled it. (Finally,) she threw away the banana and ate the peel.

103

Proofreading Practice
Writing Sequence Words

As you read the story below, you will find that sequence words have been left out. Use clue words like **first**, **next**, **then**, and **finally** to show the sequence in the story.

Teacher for the Day

If I were a teacher for the day, this is what I would do. ^First I would put a basket of candy and gum just inside the door and let the students take as much as they wanted when they arrived.

^Then, I would let everyone pick a seat beside a friend. ^Next, We would go outside to recess and play games.

^Then, We would go on a field trip to a circus. After the field trip, we would eat cookies and ice cream.

^Finally, It would be time to go home. I would let the students take more candy out of the basket as they left the room. My students would tell me that they hoped I would be their teacher tomorrow.

104

Combining Sentences

To combine sentences that have some of the words repeated, use the repeated words only once and the word **and** to join the sentences. Remember to change the verb form to agree with the plural subject.

Maria likes to hike in the mountains.
Tanya likes to hike in the mountains.
Maria and Tanya like to hike in the mountains.

If you use **I** as part of a combined subject, do not forget to put **I** last.

I am going to summer camp.
Keith is going to summer camp.
Keith and I are going to summer camp.

Practice

Combine each set of sentences below to form one sentence. Use **and** to connect two nouns or pronouns.

1. My grandpa collects stamps. I collect stamps.
   My grandpa and I collect stamps.

2. My sister sometimes gives me stamps. My dad sometimes gives me stamps.
   My sister and dad sometimes give me stamps.

3. Rare stamps are valuable. Stamps with printing errors are valuable.
   Rare stamps and stamps with printing errors are valuable.

105

Combining Sentences

- A good writer can combine sentences in several ways. One way is to combine two sentences that have some of the words repeated. Use the repeated words only once, and use **and** or **or** to join the sentences.

Gloria washed the dishes. Gloria dried the dishes.
Gloria washed **and** dried the dishes.

Gloria could dust the furniture. Gloria could vacuum the carpet.
Gloria could dust the furniture **or** vacuum the carpet.

Practice

Combine each pair of sentences below into one sentence that has two verbs, or action words.

1. Helen Keller could not see. Helen Keller could not hear.
   Helen Keller could not see or hear.

2. Helen could read Braille. Helen could write on a special typewriter.
   Helen could read Braille and write on a special typewriter.

3. She went to high school. She graduated from Radcliffe College.
   She went to high school and graduated from Radcliffe College.

4. Helen wrote books. Helen received many honors for helping others.
   Helen wrote books and received many honors for helping others.

106

Combining Sentences

- A good writer can combine sentences in several ways. One way is to use **and** to combine sentences that have some of the words repeated so that the repeated words are used only once.

    Kenji likes apples. Kenji likes oranges.
    Kenji likes apples **and** oranges.

If more than two things are named, put a comma after each one, and add **and** before the last one.

    Veronica has a dog. Veronica has a cat. Veronica has two goldfish.
    Veronica has a dog, a cat, **and** two goldfish.

Practice

Combine each set of sentences below into one sentence.

1. Our class took a trip to New York City. Our class took a trip to Washington, D.C.
   Our class took a trip to New York City and Washington, D.C.

2. We traveled by plane. We traveled by train. We traveled by bus.
   We traveled by plane, train, and bus.

3. We saw the Empire State Building. We saw the World Trade Center. We saw the Washington Monument.
   We saw the Empire State Building, the World Trade Center, and the Washington Monument.

107

Combining Sentences

- Sometimes you can improve your writing by using one or two words in place of a whole sentence.

    Grandma baked muffins.
    They were delicious.
    Grandma baked **delicious** muffins.

- You can often combine basic information from several sentences into one sentence.

    Grandma has a garden. It is in the backyard. It is big.
    Grandma has a **big** garden **in the backyard** or Grandma has a **big, backyard** garden.

Practice

Combine each group of sentences below into one sentence.

1. Rosa is going on a trip. She is going to Dallas. The trip is short.
   Rosa is going on a short trip to Dallas.

2. She packs a suitcase. It is brown. It is big.
   She packs a big, brown suitcase.

3. Uncle Larry carries the suitcase to the car. The suitcase is heavy.
   Uncle Larry carries the heavy suitcase to the car.

4. Doug meets Rosa at the airport. Rosa is Doug's cousin.
   Doug meets his cousin Rosa at the airport.

108

Combining Sentences

- In writing, you can combine short sentences to save space and add variety. Sometimes you can improve your writing by using a phrase in place of a whole sentence.

    My birthday present was a CD player. It was from Mom and Dad.
    My birthday present from Mom and Dad was a CD player.

Practice

Combine each pair of sentences into one sentence. Use a phrase in place of one sentence.

1. Oscar went sailing. He went with Ramon.
   Oscar went sailing with Ramon.

2. They sailed east. They left from the harbor.
   They sailed east from the harbor.

3. Oscar had supplies. He stored them beneath the deck.
   Oscar stored supplies beneath the deck.

4. They docked the boat. The dock was past the cove.
   They docked the boat past the cove.

5. Oscar and Ramon had a picnic. They sat near some rocks.
   Oscar and Ramon had a picnic near some rocks.

109

Combining Sentences

Read the two sentences. Choose the important word or words from the second sentence to add to the first sentence where the ↓ is.

1. I have a new ↓ skateboard.
   It is purple and black.
   I have a new purple and black skateboard.

2. I am writing a ↓ letter to my cousin.
   It is a thank-you letter.
   I am writing a thank-you letter to my cousin.

3. We ate ↓ after the homecoming game.
   We ate hot dogs and chili.
   We ate hot dogs and chili after the homecoming game.

4. I have to study for my ↓ test.
   My test is in science.
   I have to study for my science test.

5. My sister is playing ↓ in the concert.
   She is playing the cello.
   My sister is playing the cello in the concert.

110

Sentence Building

A sentence can tell more and more. Read the sentences. Look at the underlined word or words. On the lines, write **who**, **what**, **where**, or **when** to tell what the words tell in the sentence.

On the lines, combine the sentences into one sentence.

what	The magician did <u>tricks</u>.
who	The magician did tricks <u>for the kids</u>.
where	The magician did tricks <u>at the show</u>.
when	The magician did tricks <u>yesterday</u>.

<u>The magician at the show yesterday did tricks for the kids.</u>

what	I ate cake <u>and ice cream</u>.
who	I ate cake and ice cream <u>with my friends</u>.
where	I ate cake and ice cream <u>at the party</u>.
when	I ate cake and ice cream <u>this afternoon</u>.

<u>I ate cake and ice cream at the party with my friends this afternoon.</u>

what	The mother bought a <u>dress</u>.
who	The mother bought a dress <u>for her baby</u>.
where	The mother bought a dress <u>at the Little Bear Shop</u>.
when	The mother bought a dress <u>yesterday</u>.

<u>The mother bought a dress for her baby at the Little Bear Shop yesterday.</u>

111

Sentence Building

Write a word or words on each line to make the sentences tell more and more. Draw a picture of the last sentence.

My _____ Who? _____ and I went to a _____ What? _____ .

My _____ Who? _____ and I went to a _____ What? _____ at the _____ Where? _____ .

My _____ Who? _____ and I went to a _____ What? _____ at the _____ Where? _____
_____ When? _____ .

Answers and pictures will vary.

112

Sentence Building

Read the sentence parts. Write a word on each line to make the sentence tell more. Draw a picture of the last sentence.

1. We traveled _____ How? _____ .

2. We traveled _____ How? _____ to see _____ Who or what? _____ .

3. We traveled _____ How? _____ to see _____ Who or what? _____ last _____ When? _____ .

4. We traveled _____ How? _____ to see _____ Who or what? _____ last _____ When? _____ at the _____ Where? _____ .

5. We traveled _____ How? _____ to see _____ Who or what? _____ last _____ When? _____ at the _____ Where? _____ because _____ Why? _____ .

Answers and pictures will vary.

113

Using Good Letter Form

Here is a letter written in good form.

Heading →
Greeting →
Body →
Closing →
Signature →

June 8, 2002

Dear Erin,
    Would you like to keep my pet snake for the summer? I can't take him to camp with me. His name is Sneaky. He likes to curl up in my pocket. Please let me know if you want him.
                    Your friend,
                    Becky

Look carefully at the five parts of the letter above. Then answer these questions.

1. What is in the heading? <u>the date</u>

2. Where do you see commas? <u>in the date, after the greeting and closing</u>

3. Besides the first words of sentences, what words begin with capital letters?
<u>June, Dear, Erin, Sneaky, Your, Becky</u>

4. What part gives the writer's name? <u>the signature</u>

114

Using Good Letter Form

On the lines below, write these letter parts in good form. Put them in the right places. Use capital letters and commas.

june 13, 2002

dear becky

I'd love to take care of Sneaky. When can I get him?

your friend

erin

June 13, 2002

Dear Becky,

I'd love to take care of Sneaky. When can I get him?

Your friend,

Erin

115

Proofreading Practice
Friendly Letter

As you read the letter below, you will notice that there are errors in verb agreement, capitalization, and punctuation. Practice using proofreading marks to correct the errors. Use the proofreading marks on page 6 if you need help.

July 18, 2002

dear mom and dad
love   am   learned
I loves Funtime Camp! I is having a great time. I've learn
                                            ride
how to paddle a canoe without tipping it over. I can rides a
      bait   caught
horse, and I baits my own fishing hook. I catched four sunfish
the other day, but we threw them back because they needed
grow
to grew.
    sing   tell
At night we sings songs around the campfire and tells
                        ate
stories. Last night I eated six roasted marshmallows!
    tell
I'll telled you everything when you come to pick me up.

love
Doug

116

Writing a Thank-You Letter

It is good to say thank-you when someone does something nice for you or gives you a present. One way to say thank-you is to write a letter.

Maria liked the birthday present Uncle José gave her. She wrote this letter.

July 14, 2002

Dear Uncle José,
    The magic set you gave me is great. I practice with it every day after school. Now I can make a coin disappear. Soon I hope to make my brother disappear. Can you come over to see my magic show real soon?

            Your niece,
            Maria

Check the ways Maria lets her uncle know she likes his gift.

✔ She says she likes it.

✔ She tells how she uses it.

___ She says it isn't special.

✔ She invites him to share the fun.

Write On Your Own

Think of someone you'd like to thank. Write that person a letter on a separate sheet of paper. Here are some things you might thank someone for: driving you somewhere, making you something good to eat, telling you stories, being your friend.

117

Addressing Envelopes

Now that you have learned how to write a letter, you need to learn how to address an envelope. In the upper right corner of the envelope, write your name. Below your name, write your street address. The next line should include your city, state, and Zip code. In the center of the envelope, write the name of the person to whom you are writing. On the line below the person's name, write that person's street address followed by the person's city, state, and Zip code. Remember to capitalize the names of people and places. Also notice the comma placed between the city and state.

Miss Angela Jones
3434 Maple Drive
Columbus, OH 12345

Mr. and Mrs. David Smith
2642 Newberry Street
Indianapolis, IN 67890

Look at the envelope below. Correct the capitalization and punctuation. Use the envelope above to help you.

dr. justin cook
1928 riverbend road
jonesboro ak 32145

ms. patricia nilson
709 fisher street
austin tx 78438

118

NOTES

NOTES

NOTES

NOTES